STARLIGHT DREAMS

STARLIGHT HOLLOW
BOOK 2

YASMINE GALENORN

A Nightqueen Enterprises LLC Publication

Published by Yasmine Galenorn

PO Box 2037, Kirkland WA 98083-2037

STARLIGHT DREAMS

A Starlight Dreams Novel

Copyright © 2024 by Yasmine Galenorn

First Electronic Printing: 2024 Nightqueen Enterprises LLC

First Print Edition: 2024 Nightqueen Enterprises

Cover Art & Design: Ravven

Art Copyright: Yasmine Galenorn

Editor: Elizabeth Flynn

A Nightqueen Enterprises LLC Publication

Published in the United States of America

ACKNOWLEDGMENTS

Thanks to my usual crew: Samwise, my husband, Andria, and Jennifer. Without their help, I'd be swamped. To the women who have helped me find my way in indie, you're all great, and thank you to everyone. To my wonderful cover artist, Ravven, for the beautiful work she's done, and to my editor, Elizabeth, who helps me keep my ellipses under control—thank you both.

Also, my love to my furbles, who keep me happy. My most reverent devotion to Mielikki, Tapio, Ukko, Rauni, and Brighid, my spiritual guardians and guides. My love and reverence to Herne, and Cernunnos, and to the Fae, who still rule the wild places of this world. And a nod to the Wild Hunt, which runs deep in my magick, as well as in my fiction.

You can find me through my website at **Galenorn.com** and be sure to sign up for my **newsletter** to keep updated on all my latest releases! You can find my advice on writing, discussions about the books, and general ramblings on my **YouTube channel**. If you liked this book, I'd be grateful if you'd leave a review—it helps more than you can think.

January 2024
Brightest Blessings,
-The Painted Panther-
-Yasmine Galenorn-

WELCOME TO STARLIGHT DREAMS

Welcome to Starlight Hollow, a small town on Hood Canal, Washington, where dreams become nightmares, and nightmares become reality.

I'm Elphyra, the Witch of the Wild. I live in Starlight Hollow, a magical small town on the west side of Hood Canal, Washington. The town is filled with people who need magical help and advice, some tea, or a shoulder to confide in. They come to me, and I do what I can to help them and to protect the town.

Bree, my best friend, has started to notice a strange energy. She feels like she's being watched. We discover an old graveyard near her house and the trouble seems to be emanating from there. At first I think it's a ghost, but then we discover it's something far more dangerous—a force that brings up a past that both Bree and I have forgotten.

I'm going to need help, so I call on Faron Collinsworth, the King of the Olympic Wolf Pack. Faron's one of the only people who can help me go up against the stalker trying to destroy my best friend. Unfortunately, our attempts to save

Bree lands us on the stalker's hit list, and now our lives are in danger as well.

CHAPTER ONE

Breaking News! The Ripper Strikes Again!

I STARED AT THE HEADLINE ON MY LAPTOP. THE *STARLIGHT Hollow Monitor* wasn't making matters any easier for the sheriff, that was for sure. With a sigh, I read:

On the evening of August 12, a fifth victim of the Starlight Hollow Ripper was found down by Dabob Bay, in a patch of scotch broom. Rain Masters, a local fisherman, found the remains of Sandra Price, a tourist from Augusta, Maine, while taking his dog for a walk.

Price was visiting her sister in Port Townsend and had driven down to Starlight Hollow the morning of August 12. Her sister, Abigail Johnson, says that Price

1

had set out to go sightseeing on her own. When she
didn't return by seven P.M., she called the police.

Sheriff Daisy Parker urges everyone to remain calm
but asks people to avoid going into any secluded area
alone. If anyone has any information regarding this
crime, please contact her department immediately.

———————————————————————

I sighed. The only good news regarding the case was that
Faron Collinsworth's lieutenant, Elroy Zastratha, was off the
suspect list. After the scare of being considered a potential
murderer, Elroy had taken pains to always have an alibi. In
fact, he was hanging around with friends so much that he was
beginning to annoy them. And then there was the fact that
the last three murders had happened when there was no way
he could have done it.

"Breakfast?" Fancypants asked, flying down from the top
of the china hutch. The dragonette had grown in spirit during
the past month, though not much in size. But he was
ensconced in my life now and it felt like he had always been
with me. He landed on the table beside me. "You're up early,"
he added.

"Yeah, I couldn't sleep. I woke up at seven-thirty and
decided to get dressed and take a walk. Great-grandma
Morgance is driving down today to stay for a while."

My great-grandmother had shown up the second week of
August and, other than a phone call, I hadn't had a chance to
see her yet. In fact, I'd only met her once—when I was five
and my father died. She'd flown over from Scotland for the
memorial service and the cord cutting ceremony.

I didn't remember much about that day, or about her
except that she had flame red hair like I did, and she was
both beautiful and terrifying. I wasn't sure whether she

2

seemed so imposing because I was five years old and had lost my father, or whether it was an actual memory.

"Is your mother coming with her?" Fancypants had already met my mother. I'd finally allowed Catharine to come visit when I had my cast on. She'd been so worried that I couldn't refuse her. I loved my mother, but we butted heads. She still wasn't happy that I'd relocated from Port Towsend to Starlight Hollow, a forty-five-minute drive away.

"I don't think so. From the subtext of my mother's messages, I don't think they're getting along well. Great-grandma never objected to the marriage, but she and my mother are very different." I pushed back my empty latte mug and stretched. "What do you want for breakfast?"

"Sausage? Eggs?" Fancypants daintily licked his paws. Dragonettes cleaned themselves like a cat, except they had more mobility with that long slinky neck. "By the way, the top of your china hutch needs a good dusting."

"How about I give you a dustcloth and you do it?" I opened the fridge and pulled out the sausages and a carton of eggs. Dragonettes ate a lot during their first year, and he ate more than I would for breakfast. Which was saying something, given I could pack it away.

"Oh, shoo. I don't do—"

I snorted. "*Housework?* That's all well and good if you decide to run off to the wilds, but if you live under my roof—"

"*You live by my rules,*" Fancypants said with a huff. Steam puffed from his nostrils. He'd finally learned how to prevent accidental flaming hiccups. Now most of his automatic reflexes simply produced steam, which cut down on the fire risk.

"Exactly. Here." I handed him a microfiber washcloth from the counter. "Go dust while I cook."

He gave me the stink eye, but he took the cloth and flew up to the top of the china hutch. I turned back to the stove, where I tossed fourteen sausage links in a pan over medium heat—six for me, eight for him. I whipped up six eggs and added some grated cheese. I'd start them when the sausages were ready.

As I stared out the window, my phone dinged. It was my best friend, Bree Loomis.

HEY, I HAVE A QUESTION. DO YOU HAVE TIME TO COME OVER AND CHECK SOMETHING OUT? I DON'T KNOW HOW TO EXPLAIN IT, BUT SOMETHING'S GOING ON THAT'S MAKING ME NERVOUS.

I glanced at the clock. It was eight-thirty.

CAN I COME OVER AT NINE AFTER I EAT BREAKFAST? ARE YOU AT WORK? MY GREAT-GRANDMOTHER WILL BE COMING TODAY FROM PORT TOWNSEND AT NOON.

SURE. I'LL BE A LITTLE LATE TO WORK TODAY. I DON'T OPEN TILL TEN ANYWAY, AND IT TAKES ME TEN MINUTES MAX TO DRIVE DOWN TO THE SHOP. SEE YOU IN HALF AN HOUR, AND THANKS.

I turned the sausages, then added water and covered them to finish steaming them. Bree was always so levelheaded and capable that any time I sensed something amiss in her world, I worried. Hell, I worried enough when she led expeditions out into the wilderness.

I scrambled our eggs and divided them onto two plates—one Fancypants's special plate, and one my own. After adding the sausages, and two pieces of toast each, I set them on the table. "Breakfast awaits, your highness!"

He peeked over the edge of the china hutch, a dust bunny attached to the top of his head. I started to laugh and he frowned, then flew down to land by his plate.

"And what's so funny?"

"You've become one with the dust!" I snapped a quick picture and then turned the phone so he could see it.

"Oh good heavens." He hurried to wipe off the dust, chuckling. "I don't need a meeting of the minds with lint." His eyes lit up as he saw his plate. "Ooo! That looks good, thank you."

He rubbed his hands together and then flew over to the sink and washed them before returning to the table to eat. He was a fastidious little creature, far more prim and proper than I was, but somehow we worked together. It had been an interesting six weeks or so, watching him grow into his personality. At first, he'd been new to the world and mostly asking questions, but now he seemed fully acclimated. It was easy to imagine him wearing a bowler hat and carrying a walking stick.

Our bond had grown, too, and now, I couldn't imagine being without him. I cherished the fact that Fancypants had chosen me, and I was determined to live up to the honor.

"I'm headed over to Bree's in about twenty minutes. Do you want to go along?"

We had tried to keep Fancypants's existence private, but that hadn't lasted long. So, we were cautious, and he seldom went out with me.

There were wicked men in the world willing to pay a high price for a dragonette. But most of the captured creatures died when the poacher tore them away from their bond mate. Dragonettes in the wild were rare and they chose their people, not the other way around. Trying to force a bond on a dragonette was akin to mind-rape. Usually, the dragonette perished under such circumstances.

Several of my customers had seen him, and word spread, and now most of Starlight Hollow knew that Elphyra MacPherson, the owner of the newly opened Silver Thorns— a magical apothecary—had bonded with an earth dragonette.

"All right. I like Bree and I feel safe at her house," he said.

"I know, and I'm glad, especially since she's my best friend. Eat while I go turn on the sprinklers." I headed out the kitchen door and over to the raised herb beds.

The plants were thriving, burgeoning out of their beds as though I'd pumped them full of growth hormone. They felt happy and content, although I could sense they were thirsty. We were in the hottest month of the year and, while the temperatures on Hood Canal seldom rose above eighty during August, the plants still needed regular watering. I set the sprinkler where it would hit all four beds and turned it on. Then I turned on the drip irrigation hose that ran through the little kitchen garden I'd also planted and headed inside.

Fancypants was ready to go. I grabbed my purse and keys and, locking the door behind us, slid into my car. The Chevy Equinox was midnight blue—one of my favorite colors—and it handled the terrain around the Olympic Peninsula with ease. Fancypants flew into the back and settled down. As I started the ignition and eased down the long, graveled drive to Oak Leaf Road, I thought back to how my life had changed in eight months. Hell, even in the past two months.

MY NAME'S ELPHYRA MACPHERSON, and I'm a witch. I moved to Starlight Hollow, Washington—a town of three thousand people on the edge of Dabob Bay—around eight months ago. Originally from Port Townsend, which was three times the size of Starlight Hollow, I left my home and plans behind after my fiancé was ruthlessly murdered by a vampire while I was forced to watch. The trauma of sitting there help-lessly, watching the torture, and then watching the rats move in for the remains left me with a serious case of PTSD.

Unable to face life in the town where the love of my life had been murdered, I packed my bags, took the trust fund that my father had left me, and bought three acres and a cottage in Starlight Hollow. I moved, applied for my business license to open up the shop of my dreams, and turned my back on the past. Or rather, I *tried* to. But the past has a way of coming back to haunt you if you don't have closure, and my past intrudes in my thoughts every day.

Being near Bree helps—she's been my best friend since high school. My neighbor May, a lovely old witch woman, and her son Bran, are delightful. May's become a role model, and Bran and I date occasionally. I'm also dating Faron Collinsworth, the King of the Olympic Wolf Pack.

Balancing the two is proving difficult, but I like them both and they know about each other. Unless something happens to disrupt that delicate balance, I'm good with the way things are. I hadn't thought of dating until they came into the scene, but when the spirit of my fiancé showed up and told me to move on, to let him go, I finally faced the facts: the future isn't waiting for me to be ready. It's coming regardless of how I feel.

BREE LIVED about two miles away on Salmonberry Drive, a side street off Thoroughfare Drive. Thoroughfare Drive was the main street that ran north to south through Starlight Hollow.

True to its name, Salmonberry Drive had several empty lots covered with salmonberries, and I had managed to gather enough to make twenty pints of jam during May and June. The bright orange berries were endemic throughout the Pacific Northwest. Now, in mid-August, the bushes sat berryless, but their foliage was still green and bushy with leaves.

The canes were covered with prickles, but they weren't as painful as blackberry thorns.

I passed three lots on either side, pulling into the fourth driveway on the left. Bree's house was a single-story house—a rambler. A large shed sat to the left of the house against the fence dividing her lot from her northside neighbor. The house was painted a pale gray, and the yard was spotless. Bree loved doing yard work, and she kept her lawn and gardens immaculate. It wasn't a cookie-cutter suburban lawn that looked like AstroTurf. No, the lawn was neat, with patches of flowers laid out across the sprawling grass. A large weeping willow filled the front yard, giving a southern gothic feel to the house.

I rang the bell and instantly heard barking. That had to be Atlas, her black Labrador retriever, and Oscar, her husky. Both were loud but well-trained, and in good physical shape. She took them with her when she was out scouting locations for expeditions, and she also took them with her during the actual trips. They provided an extra measure of protection, and generally made her female clients feel safer on the women-only expeditions.

A moment later, I heard her telling the dogs to get back, and she opened the door and waved me in. Atlas and Oscar knew me, but they weren't sure about Fancypants, who was sitting on my shoulder. He flew up toward the ceiling and they took off, barking their silly heads off.

"Sorry, I didn't think about the dogs' reaction to Fancypants. I can ask him to—"

"Don't worry. They'll adapt, but for now, let me put them into the backyard." She paused, then said, "That's what I wanted to ask you about, anyway."

"The backyard or the dogs?" I asked, following her through the living room. Bree had an eclectic design aesthetic. Her snowboard hung on one wall, next to a couple framed shots of her when she had been twenty, when she had won the Rainier Aerial Freestyle Competition. The next year, she had crashed during a practice to uphold her title. Instead of one bone breaking, it had been seven fractures in her left hip, leg, and ankle. Bree had recovered but was never able to compete again.

Against the other wall, shelves covered the wall from floor to ceiling. They contained neat, tidy rows of books as well as a few knickknacks. It looked like she had raided Target or Walmart and stocked up on minimalist vases, single silk roses, and an assortment of river rocks.

She whistled twice. Both dogs immediately quieted and sat down. She whistled again, then said, "Yard." The dogs stood and trotted into the kitchen. We followed, to find them sitting by the back door. Bree opened it. They continued to wait, although they looked like they were straining to keep still. "Attention!" The dogs stood. "Go!"

They bounced out, yipping as they raced around the yard, chasing each other.

"Do your neighbors ever complain?" I asked. "About the noise?"

"I have one neighbor to worry about. To the left is a berry lot, to the right everybody's dead. Across the street, Mrs. Clary is deaf as they come. To her left and right, the neighbors also have dogs, and they don't complain."

Bree lived next to a graveyard. It was small—about two acres—and overgrown. Nobody took care of the graves anymore. It had been established sometime in the late 1800s and most of the inhabitants had taken up residence before 1950. Their families were gone—dead or moved on—leaving the headstones as the only proof that at some time, the dead had truly belonged to the living.

"Do you have any crackers?" Fancypants asked.

"You're kidding. You're still hungry after that breakfast I fixed?"

He nodded, rubbing his belly.

Bree crooked her finger. "Come on, I'll get some for you."

Fancypants followed her back into the kitchen. A moment later she returned without him. "He's busy eating a box of Ritz crackers."

"I love those," I said. "So, what's going on? Your texts sounded worried."

"I am worried," Bree said, motioning for me to take a seat on the back steps with her. She had a small porch, barely large enough to act as a landing for the five steps leading to the yard. But the steps were wide enough for two people to sit on.

"Why? What happened?"

"First, can you sit here for a bit and then tell me if you sense anything?" She was so concerned that it worried me. Bree could take care of herself and if something happened to interrupt that confidence, it was time to be worried.

I nodded. "All right."

I held out my hands. As I let my conscious mind drift into a trance state, I moved through the layers making up the world around me. There was the conscious layer—the mundane layer, so to speak—that we all lived in. This was the layer where we went to work, met with friends, shopped, and drove and interacted with all that seemed concrete.

Below that were other levels of existence.

Next came the level permeating nature, where the elements settled into form: into the ocean, lakes, and rivers; into the volcanoes, wildfires, and the warmth of the sun; into the mountains, plants, and animals; and into the gusting breezes, the tornadoes, the very air that filled our lungs.

And there was the shadow layer—existing on the ethereal and astral planes, where dark and light were muted into so many shades of gray that it was impossible to count them. Here were monsters of the mind that could also destroy the body, nameless nebulous forms that offered us strength, or sucked the life out of us. Here lurked the Shadow People, and the creatures that came in from the far reaches of the void. And here were the Celestial Beings, who could wound mortals with their blinding light as easily as the Shadow People did with their inky darkness.

And yet, another level—the level of spirits who were moving toward the Veil. Here were the ghosts waiting for closure, the haunts who were so angry over losing their lives that they couldn't see all that awaited them on the other side of the Veil. Here were the undead—the vampires who lived in a perpetual twilight.

And so, the count went on. How many layers existed? I didn't know. But they all belonged to the web that stretched through the universe to connect everything and everyone. And on that web were intersections where we could see into the vast realms that spread beyond time and space.

I let my vision drift. Figures appeared in the graveyard. I could see them easily from where I sat, but none stood out to me. They wandered around the grounds, stopping now and then to add another spirit to their group. After a few minutes I shifted my focus, listening to the light breeze, to the birds announcing their plans for the day. The heat was coming—it would be warm later, and any rain was a long ways away. No storms lay on our horizon, only a procession of summer days.

I moved on to the animals, but there were no surprises there, either—and no sense that anything was up. Except... the dogs stood on alert, even while they played. I walked over to where they were tussling over a knotted towel. They looked at me expectantly, so I knelt and called them over.

As they crowded in, eager to play, I stroked their backs and tried to sense what they were focused on. I found myself drifting into their thoughts. At first I saw warm, fuzzy images of Bree, then their treats and toys, of each other...there was even a cozy thought of me. But beneath all that was worry—concern. Beneath all their happy thoughts was a low-level awareness of being watched. Of needing to protect the yard more than usual. Shadows crept around the perimeter of the yard.

Atlas and Oscar suddenly bayed as a whirlwind sense of danger broke through their thoughts and splashed against me like a cold shower of water. I did what I could to find out what was going on, but the fear was all that I could latch on to, and after a few moments I stopped. I was disconcerting the dogs, and I didn't want to stress them out.

"What is it?" Bree said, walking over beside me.

I threw the knotted towel and the dogs bounded after it, once again their happy-go-lucky selves. "I don't know, but the dogs are picking up on some sort of danger. It's coming from the graveyard. So, yeah, there's something out there, focused on your house. You need to be cautious until we pinpoint who's behind it and whether it's deliberately directed at you, or you're just in the crosshairs."

"Wonderful," Bree said, crossing her arms. "That's the last thing I need—an invisible voyeur." She glanced around, uneasily. "What should I do?"

"For now, keep alert. Lock your doors. I'll help you ward your house. I think that's all you can do." I hated saying that, but it was true. The cops wouldn't laugh her off—they knew all about the invisible worlds around us—but neither would they be able to do anything. It was hard enough prosecuting a corporeal stalker, let alone an elusive spirit.

As she played with the dogs, I turned back to the grave-yard. I needed to explore it, but I didn't want to until I had someone with me, and I knew Bree didn't want to go. Regardless of the strides I'd made, I was still terrified that I might run into a vampire.

Bree and I returned to the kitchen, where I found Fancypants, lounging in a food coma. He burped, apologized for eating the entire box of crackers, and then followed me out to my car. It was time to get going on the day.

CHAPTER TWO

BY THE TIME FANCYPANTS AND I ARRIVED HOME, I WAS
swinging between speculating what was skulking around
Bree's house and planning lunch and dinner for my great-
grandma. Although she said she'd eat anything, I had my
doubts. She was very much the Dowager Countess of
Downton Abbey, only modernized.

"What do you think is going over at Bree's?" Fancypants
asked. "The dogs were upset."

"Yes, they were, weren't they? But I couldn't pinpoint
anything, except that whatever it is, it seems to be concen-
trated in the graveyard. I should go search through it, except
that I have to get ready for Grams's visit. I'll try to make time
tomorrow to walk through it. Want to come?"

"Your idea of showing a dragonette a good time is to drag
him through an active cemetery?" Fancypants snorted.

"Don't sweat it, you don't have to come." I rolled my eyes.

"Thank you. I really don't enjoy hanging out with ghosts.
They tend to be a nasty bunch, on the whole. Especially
human ghosts. Cat spirits I can hang with. Dog spirits—
they're usually all right. Even bird spirits can be fun. But no, I

don't want to go boogie in the graveyard," he said. "So, what do you want me to do around here?"

I glanced around. Dragonettes weren't great at house-work, although the stunt with the dusting earlier made me think he could handle that. "If you want to, you could help me by dusting anything and everything you see that needs it. I thought I'd gotten the house relatively clean, but after seeing the dust from that hutch today…"

"Same cloth?"

"Yes, and I have more, if it gets too dirty."

Fancypants picked up the dustcloth and flew off into the kitchen. I glanced around. While the house was already tidy, I straightened the throw pillows on the sofa and rocking chair. After clearing the coffee table of the usual accumulation of miscellaneous stuff, I did the same for the foyer table near the door. A glance out the window reminded me that I needed to turn off the sprinklers, so I ran outside to do so. While I was there, I cut a few stems of mint—enough to make fresh tea—and then turned back to the house.

My phone rang, startling me. I juggled the herbs as I glanced at the screen. *Faron.* Blushing, I answered. "Hey, what's up?"

"I'm at work, but I was thinking about you," Faron said. "Want to grab dinner tonight?"

I hesitated. Given my great-grandma was coming to stay for a while, I didn't want to make plans for her first night here.

"I can't, I'm sorry. Remember? I told you my great-grand-mother's arriving this afternoon. She's been staying with my mother for a week and now she's coming down to see me."

"That's right," Faron said. "I remember. All right, but what about tomorrow? I'd like to meet her."

I froze, sinking onto one of the chairs on my patio. "*You* want to meet my great-grandmother? I don't know if that's a

15

good idea." I wanted plenty of time to get her used to the idea that I was dating a wolf shifter. Witches and wolf shifters had issues, and I didn't want to get into it with her yet.

Faron was silent for a moment, then said, "Oh...right. I forgot." After another pause, he changed the subject. "Did you know that Sheriff Parker has asked for my help in the murder case? Given the coroner thinks the suspect is a shifter —he's not so sure about a *wolf* shifter anymore, but it could be any number of types—the sheriff wants to know if my men will join the patrol force, keeping watch through the town. They enlisted the Quinault Forest Bear Sleuth to help them. We're going to be instituting night watchmen duties, in groups of three."

"How do you feel about that?" I asked, heading back indoors.

"Rather odd, given she was eyeing Elroy as a suspect for a while. But he's made peace with her, and so I decided to take the high road and agree." His voice dropped. "I wish I could see you today. I miss you."

It had been almost a week since I'd seen Faron and, while we weren't exclusive, our conversations had been growing deeper. We were getting more physical, although I hadn't been open to climbing in bed with him yet.

"I miss you too," I said. "But now, I have to go. I'll try to introduce the subject that we're dating to my great-grandma, but I can't promise how she'll react."

"Are you going to introduce her to Bran?" Faron's voice dropped, irritated.

I hesitated. *Land mine territory.* "I don't know. See you later." I ended the call. If I introduced Bran to my great-grandma, but not Faron, Faron would be pissed. The pair had developed a rivalry over me, but they were keeping it civil. They knew I'd kick both of them to the curb if their antagonism turned physical.

I carried the mint inside and washed it, setting it on the counter to dry. Fancypants had finished dusting. I could tell, which meant the room had needed more care than I thought.

"I dropped the dustcloth in the laundry basket. You need to wash it before it's capable of being used again—" he paused. "What's wrong?"

I shrugged. "Faron wants me to introduce him to my great-grandmother."

Fancypants snorted, steam rising from his nostrils. "*Oh, does he?* I'd like to be the dragonfly on the wall for that conversation."

"Not me. Anyway, I'll wash the dishes from breakfast. What should I give her for lunch? I'm not sure if she takes tea, or what. While she's written to me a few times, I don't know much about her." But before I could do anything, the doorbell rang. It had to be her.

I glanced down at my outfit. I was wearing a pair of black denim shorts—not so short they showed my goodies but short enough, and a hunter green halter top. I had paired the outfit with a pair of handmade Roman gladiator-style sandals. Each strap around my calf had its own buckle, though the back strip of leather up my leg had a cleverly hidden zipper so it wouldn't take me forever to get them on and off. The front strip had diamond cutouts where the straps crisscrossed, and a flip-flop like toe strap. I'd pulled my hair into a long ponytail, and my makeup was good.

"I guess I'm ready," I told Fancypants, taking a deep breath.

He winked at me. "You look good. For a biped."

Laughing, I answered the door.

GREAT-GRANDMA MORGANCE WASN'T EXACTLY what I had expected. I'd seen pictures of her, but they were from when she was young. Tall and with a sturdy, trim build, she still had long red hair like mine, though hers had faded some. She wore it caught up in a low chignon, so neat and tidy that it gleamed under the sun. Her hair was long and straight, compared to mine, which was long and wavy.

Great-grandma was over a hundred and twenty, but she didn't look a day over eighty. Witches had a longer lifespan than humans, though we usually didn't live as long as shifters. But we could reach upward of a hundred and seventy with good habits and some luck. So, Great-grandma still had a ways to go.

She was dressed in a black bouclé skirt suit. The blazer had gold military buttons and patch pockets and came down to her hips. The skirt was a simple pencil skirt. Beneath the blazer, she was wearing a cream-colored satin shirt with a Celtic brooch at the neck. Atop her head, she wore a wide-brimmed hat to match. I felt so underdressed that I might as well have been wearing just my bra and panties.

She gave me the once-over, her dark eyes flashing. With a hint of a smile, she held out her arms and I moved in, but she simply air-kissed me on both cheeks and then stood back, keeping hold of my hands.

"You've grown up to be a pretty thing, I have to say." Her voice was firm. She squeezed my hands and let go. "Well, are you going to invite me in?"

Flustered, I scrambled out of the way. "Of course. Please come in, Grams." That was my nickname for her whenever we emailed.

"Thank you." She wandered around the living room, inspecting the bookshelves, the furniture, and whatever else her gaze fell on.

"Are your bags in the car?" I asked. Grams had rented a car and driver. "I can get them."

"Ask the driver to bring them in, please. I assume you can drive and that's your Equinox out there?"

"Of course."

"Good. Please give the driver this." She handed me a credit card. "Tell him to add a 15 percent gratuity and that I'll call when I next need his services. I'll be in the kitchen, putting your kettle on for tea. I assume you have a tea kettle?"

I smothered a laugh. "Yeah, it's on the stove." Grams was certainly imperious. But that fit what I knew of her. I headed outside and leaned down by the driver's window. He was sitting there, checking his phone, looking vaguely bored.

"Hey, can you bring in her luggage? Here's the credit card and I'm going to add a 15 percent tip. And she'll call you when she needs you next." As I glanced at the fee schedule, it looked about right—$140 for a round trip from Port Townsend. In Seattle, it would be an hourly rate, but over here where rush hour traffic had little meaning, TownCars Limited, a popular car service in the area, charged by the actual trip.

"Surely will, ma'am." The driver ran Grams's credit card through, then handed the scanner to me so I could add the tip and approve it. I did so, accepting the receipt. He hopped out of the Town Car and retrieved the three suitcases and three hat boxes from the back, following me into the house. I showed him the guest room and he set the luggage there, then tipped his hat and left.

As he pulled out of the driveway, I realized that there was no going back. Grams was here with me for a couple weeks, come good or ill.

"First things first, my girl," Grams said once the driver was gone. Her brogue was heavy, but I could understand her.

19

I had a knack with dialects. "Introduce me to your little friend. He scared the color away from my cheeks when he flew up behind me." She still stared at me impassively, but I caught a twinkle of laughter in her voice.

I cleared my throat. "I'm sorry. I should have told you about him, but I haven't even told Mom yet and..."

"And you didn't want to talk in front of her," Grams said. "Well then, formally introduce us, my bairn. I won't tell your mother unless you want me to." She took off her hat and set it on the side table, then unbuttoned her blazer and handed it to me. After hanging it in the foyer closet, I motioned for her to follow me into the kitchen.

Fancypants was sitting on the table, playing with some of the mint leaves I'd brought in earlier. He jumped when he saw me, trying to hide them behind his back.

"Hey, those are for tea. I told you to ask before you touch my herbs!"

"I can't help it. Mint is like catnip for me. I love the way it smells...and tastes..." Fancypants let out a satisfied chirp, and I rolled my eyes.

"Yes, yes, you love mint. Fancypants, I want you to meet my great-grandmother, Morgance. She'll be staying with us for a while. Grams, meet Fancypants." I turned to my great-grandmother. "I'll have to get more mint. I was going to make tea for us. I forgot about his mint obsession."

Grams cracked a smile. "I see. Well, save yourself the trouble. I don't like mint tea. I'm partial to black currant tea, and strong black tea." She turned to Fancypants. "Hello, fair dragonette." After a pause, she added, "My great-grand-daughter actually named you *Fancypants?*"

"Unfortunately, yes. At first it annoyed me but now, I'm rather taken with it. I bid you welcome to our household. I trust you had a fair journey?" Fancypants had a degree of respect in his voice that I seldom heard.

"Oh, it was bumpy. Up, down, all around, but what can you expect when you're 30,000 feet up in the air? At least we don't ride on brooms. That would chafe anyone's inner thighs." She laughed, then, robust and full.

My jaw dropped. "I'm sorry?" Hearing my great-grand-mother talk about anybody's inner thighs seemed so out of character that it took me aback.

"Don't mistake formality for having no sense of humor, my girl. Anyway, as I was saying, it was a bumpy ride and I'm grateful we made it here safely." She sat down at the table. "Have you nothing to offer your guest? My *tummok's* rumbling."

" 'Tummok'?" Fancypants asked.

Grams laughed softly. "It's a word Malcolm, my grandson —Elphyra's father—used when he was young. He couldn't pronounce 'stomach' and for the first eight years of his life, he pronounced it 'tummok.' I picked up the habit. I still use it because it always makes me smile."

I remembered little about my father, and I certainly didn't remember this story, but it made me feel closer to Grams. "Father's death scarred my mother. I never wanted to make her unhappy by asking about him. Now, I barely remember what his name was and what he looked like."

Grams sat back in her chair, hands in her lap. "I always liked your mother, dear, but she's not a strong woman. Not like you. She tries, but she doesn't have the stoicism to manage most of life's 'slings and arrows of outrageous fortune,' to quote the Bard."

I couldn't argue with her there. Catharine had a sensitive nature, which wasn't a bad thing. But it made life hard on her. She had shut down when my father died, and had left me to fend on my own, emotionally. At the age of five, I had taught myself to pretend that I was all right. And that was how I managed until I met Rian and he opened up my softer side.

21

But when he died, it hit me so hard that I had ricocheted, spiraling into trauma, and it felt like I was still fighting to claw my way out of that abyss.

"What are you thinking about?" Grams asked. "You have the most peculiar look on your face."

I thought for a moment before answering her. "I wish I'd been more middle of the road when Rian died. He exposed my vulnerable side, and I let him. I couldn't hide how much I loved him and I wanted the world to know how happy we were. But I also lost that resilience that guided me through my father's death. When Rian died, I tumbled…" Trying to distract myself from my thoughts, I said, "What would you like for lunch? I can make omelets or sandwiches and soup. What would you like?"

Grams didn't try to steer the conversation around again. She said, "Sandwiches and soup will be fine."

As I fixed roast beef sandwiches and vegetable soup for lunch, Grams brought out her tablet and engaged Fancypants in a game of online chess. He proved more than a match for her, which startled all of us. By the time lunch was ready, he had won the first game.

"Okay, put the game aside. Lunch is ready." I set the tray of sandwiches in the center, then set out bread-and-butter plates, two regular soup bowls, and a small crystal ramekin that would serve as a bowl for Fancypants. I ladled out the soup and then asked, "What do you want to drink, Grams?"

"Do you have lemonade?" she asked.

I poured two glasses, handing one to her. "Always. It's one of my favorite drinks."

As we ate, I realized that I was running out of things to say. I had no clue what to talk about, except about my father's life. Or magic, of course, since she was a powerful witch, known through the great Witch Houses back in the United Kingdom.

"So," she said, after finishing half a sandwich. "I imagine you're wondering what I'm doing here."

"Well, as a matter of fact, yes. I am. The last time you came to visit was when my father died." I wondered whether to tell her that I resented never getting to know her before this. I didn't resent *her*, exactly, but the circumstances and distance that kept us apart.

"I don't travel well, to be honest. But I came here because of you, my dear."

"*Me?*"

"Remember, in my note I said that trauma can skew the powers in our family in all sorts of unwelcome ways?" She picked up another half sandwich and bit into it. "These are delicious."

"Thanks. And yes, I remember. I wasn't sure what you meant."

"I'm here to explain. Over the past year, since I found out what happened to you, I thought and meditated about it, and I made a decision."

I waited, as she took another bite of her sandwich. "Yes? What did you decide?"

"I'm moving to the States so I can be near you."

Boom.

"I've bought a house in Port Townsend. I'm staying with your mother until my furniture arrives from Scotland, and then I'll settle in."

Boom. The shoe dropped, indeed!

Her words reverberating in my mind, I silently reached for another sandwich as the thoughts fluttered down to fully form themselves in my mind.

My great-grandmother was moving all the way from Scotland to live nearby. My great-grandmother wanted to keep an eye on me. My great-grandmother was going to make my mother's life a living hell, most likely. That made me both want to grimace and laugh. Catharine was no match for Grams, yet the interaction might do her a great deal of good. Grams was strong and she could teach my mother a trick or two. At the same time, she was going to probably needle my mother to distraction.

And what about you?

The thought intruded and I cleared my throat. That was a good question. *What about me? How often is she planning on visiting? How often will she wander in and complain about my lifestyle?* From the little I'd seen of her so far, Grams was perfectly capable of sweeping in and disregarding anybody who challenged her. *What if she decides she doesn't like the way I live?* All these thoughts ran through my head as I sat there.

Fancypants must have noticed my silence, because he fluttered his wings and loudly asked, "Lady Morgance—may I call you that?"

"Of course, you may, Sir Fancypants." Grams's eyes twinkled.

"Thank you. Then, Lady Morgance, can you tell me how you find the town? Do you like it here?"

I silently blessed the dragonette and took a deep breath, trying to process the information. My great-grandmother was the matriarch of the MacPherson clan and that wasn't going to change just because she was changing countries.

"Well, Port Townsend is a lovely town, though quirky. Beneath that veneer, however, there are several deep scars. It's satisfactory for my needs, though. Starlight Hollow is too steeped in the woodland for me to consider living here. I feel rather claustrophobic."

While she was speaking, I managed to get hold of myself and I flashed her a smile as she looked at me. "Well, we'll have to have a party, then, once you're moved in."

"There's no need for that. However, I do plan on hosting an afternoon tea once a month. You will be required to attend. I'll make certain it falls on one of your free days." She paused, then added, "Don't think that I don't know how worried this makes you. You're afraid I'm going to cramp your style and try to mold you in my image. While I can't promise that I won't offer advice, I'm not here to disrupt your life, my girl."

"Yes, Grams." I paused, then decided to address my worries later. "Where are you going to live? You said you bought a house?"

"I did. I bought a house on 58th Street, overlooking the water. It's not what I'm used to—it's smaller than the family home—but it will be fine for me and for whomever I hire as an assistant." Grams pushed her soup bowl back. "I'll have you up to visit once I'm settled in."

I froze. "I haven't visited Port Townsend since I moved."

Grams gave me a look that I wasn't sure I wanted to see again. "You *will* visit me there. Now, I'm old and it's time for my nap. Feel free to do whatever it is you do this time of day. When do we eat dinner? I'll want time to dress."

"Dress for dinner?" The thought of visiting Port Townsend had thrown me into a tizzy, and now she wanted me to dress for dinner. Because if *she* was dressing for dinner, it meant we were *all* going to dress.

"For heaven's sake, you aren't hard of hearing, are you?" Grams stood and, waving her cane, added, "Of course we'll dress for dinner. It's the civilized thing to do. Now, what time do we eat?"

"Six, I guess. Seven? When do you want dinner? I'm flexible." I ate when I was hungry rather than following a schedule, but Grams had always led a formal lifestyle.

"Seven will do. I'll set my alarm for four and then I'll unpack, have a wash, and be ready for the evening. Have a good afternoon, my dear. As for you, Sir Fancypants, I look forward to our next round of chess."

"And I, too, look forward to the game!" Fancypants perked up.

Grams disappeared into the living room. I peeked after her, just in time to see her vanish into the guest room and shut the door behind her. A moment later, I dropped into my seat with a deep breath. The afternoon had been exhausting. I felt like I was in a dog show, and she was the main judge. My ears weren't right, my coat wasn't shiny enough, *so many* things were found wanting.

And yet, I knew Grams loved me. She cared. I could feel the connection between us in my bones. Oddly enough, I'd never felt this with my mother, and that didn't seem right. But there it was. And here I was. And Grams was moving to Port Townsend, and everything was about to change. I carried the lunch dishes to the sink and rinsed them, then stacked them in the dishwasher.

Deciding I needed a walk, I grabbed my walking stick and slid into sneakers, then headed out, Fancypants sitting on my shoulder. Maybe May could help me process everything that had gone on. I dropped her a text and she said *Come on over*, so I steered us toward the trailhead that led through the thicket to May's house, wishing it was time for Grams to go home.

CHAPTER THREE

THE FOREST CALMED ME DOWN. EVERY TIME I FELT ON edge, if I could get to a thicket or a park and walk in silence, my feathers would unruffle. Of course, now with a serial killer on the loose, there was always a sense of trepidation that I couldn't shake. There was no reason to believe he'd avoid private property, and the thicket between May's house and mine was wooded enough to offer shelter and give him a convenient place to strike. Then again, there wouldn't be as many people out here as there would be in a park. But even that thought offered scant comfort.

Fancypants flew off my shoulder and spiraled into the air, stretching his wings. He flew ahead of me, hovering lightly about six feet off the ground.

"What does it feel like to fly?" I asked.

"Freedom. It's so freeing to be able to resist gravity. Although my wings do get tired after a while. I don't know how birds do it—flying thousands of miles when they migrate. I know they can stay aloft for months on end, and some birds are in the air most of their lives."

"Their bones are hollow," I said. "I read that it acts as

though they have extra lung capacity." I tried to imagine it—
life in the air, never touching ground. There were probably
some birds that never touched the earth a day in their lives.
The thought both boggled my mind yet made me wonder
what it would be like—to spend my life among the air
currents.

"How long can *you* stay aloft?" I asked.

"Several hours. Now, a dragonette bound to the air can
stay on the wing longer. Our connections to the elements
bind us into those spheres. If I'm traveling a long way, it's
easier for me to travel into Sescernaht and travel between the
worlds."

I nodded. Sescernaht was the space between worlds where
dragons and all their ilk gathered. It was like a wormhole
world, but dragons were the only ones who could shift into
that realm.

At that moment, we came to the border dividing May's
property from mine, and I turned onto the trail leading to her
house. May's property felt different than mine. She had
poured magic into the land for decades, and it was super
charged. While she was more of a kitchen witch, May was
still a formidable spellcaster.

The trail, like the path on my side of the thicket, led
through open grass. The yard was huge, though I
suspected that on the other side, she had less front yard
than me. Beds of roses dotted the lawn, along with a patch
of wildflowers. A large garden—easily twenty times the
size of my kitchen garden—took up a good share of the
backyard. A small orchard of fruit trees lay to our right,
farther toward the front. The pond was on the other side
of her house. During extremely cold winters, apparently it
froze over so that you could skate on it, and in summer,
while it wasn't large, the pond was big enough to splash
around in.

May was out back, weeding in her kitchen garden. I didn't see Bran anywhere.

"Hey," I said, waving to catch her attention.

She looked up. "Hey," she answered, removing the straw hat she was wearing and wiping her brow. "Let's go inside. It's starting to warm up. You want some coffee?"

I licked my lips. "Am I ever one to say no to coffee?"

She led me up the steps to the back porch and through the screen door. As she did, a fluffy, longhaired white cat raced over to her side. Gigi was May's cat, and she was a five-year-old Siberian. The cat's eyes were blue and green—two alternate colors—giving her a slightly surreal look. I leaned down and Gigi bounced over to me, rubbing against my hand as she examined me to see if I had hidden any treats.

Fancypants landed by her side and she glanced at him, then slowly headbutted him, knocking him over.

"Hey, watch the love, lady. You're sweeping me off my feet!" Fancypants gave her an awkward pat on the head, then flew up to the counter. Gigi huffed, then wandered off, shaking her tail as if to say *I didn't want your attention anyway!*

Snorting, I sat down at the table as May handed me a couple of dessert plates, then brought over an angel food cake, along with a container of sliced strawberries and a can of spray whipping cream.

"That looks delicious," I said.

"Then cut a good-size slice and go to town. I'll get the forks." As she brought the silverware I cut two slices, one for her and one for me. Then I spooned out the strawberries onto the cake and sprayed a dollop of whipped cream over it.

"So, your great-grandmother arrived?"

"Why do you think I'm here drowning myself in sugar?" I said glumly. "I'm glad she's here, but heaven help me. May, she's bought a house on the water. She's going to be living in Port Townsend now. I can't believe she decided to move all that way. I'll never be able to relax again." I stared glumly into my cake. "Faron wanted me to introduce him."

"Are you going to?" May asked, adding whipped cream to her plate.

"What do you think? He's the King of his Pack. Wolf shifters and witches—"

"Right. Maybe not the best idea, at least, not before you can warm her up to the idea." May hesitated, then said, "You can safely introduce her to Bran, though."

May had been walking a tightrope for some time. She was championing her son, of course, but she didn't want to push me and I respected her for that. She understood the nuances that went into my dating, and that I wasn't ready to make a choice.

"Right, I can do that." Truth was, I wasn't sure I *wanted* to introduce her to Bran, given the fact that we were dating, he was a witch, and he'd immediately be the right choice in my great-grandmother's mind.

"So," May said, pushing back her chair. "What do you really think is behind her moving here? Is it as simple as she says, that she wants to watch over you?"

I shook my head. "I don't think that's all of it, but it's all I'm going to drag out of her for the time being. I'll have to visit her in Port Townsend when she gets her new house together. I haven't been back since I left and I had no plans to. But she made it clear that I'm to get my ass up there at some point."

"And you don't want to."

"No, I don't." I wanted to cry, more in frustration than anything else. "I moved away from Port Townsend for several reasons. One, the memories. But two—my family. I love my mother, I really do. And my aunt and cousin. But they're so nosy. They're always prying into my business and I'm not prepared to give them that leeway any longer."

"And you think that now that your great-grandmother is living there, the pressure will increase?" May asked. She cut another slice of cake.

"I *know* it will increase. I can do battle with my mother and aunt, but with Grams involved? Not going to happen. Fighting against her decisions is like banging your head against a brick wall. Unless you unearth a battering ram—and it better be a good one—she's impenetrable."

"I look forward to meeting her," May said. "She sounds like a firebrand."

"Try a raging inferno. Anyway, I needed to clear my head so I thought I'd walk over. I went over to Bree's this morning. She has a problem, but I can't figure out what it is." I told her about the energy in the graveyard. "It's so tangible…I wanted to go take a walk through the graveyard but with Grams coming, I had to get home. And I'd rather have backup when I go, anyway."

"Your great-grandmother is a powerful witch, isn't she?" May asked.

"Yes, but do you think it's wise taking her?" As I said the words, I heard how ridiculous they sounded. Yes, my great-grandma was still capable of moving around and she was nowhere near death's door. "Would you like to come, too? I'd like for you to meet her."

"When were you thinking?"

"Well, maybe tomorrow evening? She expects dinner at seven, so around eight? In fact, why don't you come to dinner tonight? That way, you and Bran can meet her."

"That would be lovely," May said. "I'll help deflect some of her attention."

When I tried to protest, she laughed.

"I know why you're asking me and it doesn't offend me in the least. But I insist we bring Bran to the graveyard tomorrow evening. The serial killer's still on the loose and while we're powerful witches, your great-grandmother and I aren't exactly spring chickens when it comes to protecting ourselves. I know you're strong, but you can't protect all three of us, either."

I sighed. I wasn't going to try to get out of that one. She was right. "All right. Sounds good."

As I prepared to go, Fancypants buzzed May's head and then landed on her shoulder long enough to give her a little smooch on the cheek.

"Why, thank you, Fancypants!" She laughed and handed him a cookie. He flapped his wings, excited. Sometimes he really did remind me of a dog.

"Come on, Sir Fancelot, let's move." I stood. "May, would you mind bringing dessert tonight? Grams has a sweet tooth, though more for fruit than anything else."

"I'll bake a pie," she said. "What's her favorite fruit?"

"I don't know, but she was talking about peaches the other day."

"Peach pie it is," May said as she saw us to the door. She handed me a basket with a couple dozen cookies in a plastic bag in it. "Here. Since your pal here likes them, make sure he gets a couple for a treat."

As we started back through the trail, Fancypants zipped around through the trees, suddenly stopping about ten yards off the trail from me.

"Berries!" he called out.

"What kind?"

"Looks like wild raspberries," he said.

I waded through the knee-high undergrowth, brushing past the ferns and Oregon grape and vine maple to where he was hovering. Sure enough, there was a small patch of wild raspberries there, and they were ripe. I stacked the cookies to one side of the basket and sat it on the ground so I could fill the rest of the space with berries.

Fancypants, with his delicate hands and ability to fly and hover, was able to reach the berries on the top of the patch. He ate half of what he picked, but I didn't say anything. The berries were warm and they tasted like sweet sunshine. Within twenty minutes, we had filled the basket and stripped most of the bushes.

"Remember where this is," I said. "I should dig up a few canes and transplant them to the corner of the yard. I have some blackberries there, so it would be nice to have wild raspberries along with them." I picked up the basket and we headed home.

IT WAS NEARING four P.M. when we arrived home. Grams would be up soon. I put the cookies on a cake plate and covered them with the dome, to keep Fancypants from eating them all at once, and then washed the berries gently and laid them out on paper towels to dry before putting them in the fridge.

Time to plan for dinner. Having no clue what Grams liked, I decided to go with spaghetti. I had no more started sautéing the onions and garlic in the pan when someone knocked on the kitchen door. Wiping my hands on a tea towel, I answered the door. It was Bran.

"Hey, what's up?" I asked, stepping back to let him in.

"May sent me to drop off these," he said, handing me a bag. "She said you might need them."

I peeked inside the brown lunch bag. It was half full of tomatoes. Frowning, I set it on the counter. "I don't, really, but—" Then I stopped as a thought struck me. I checked the fridge. Sure enough, the bowl I kept fresh tomatoes in was empty. "Fancypants! Front and center!"

He flew in from the living room. "You rang?"

"Where did the tomatoes go and how did you get into the fridge? I know you can't open the door by yourself."

He rolled his eyes. With a melodramatic sigh, he landed on the counter and swept one arm up to brush against his forehead. "You wound me! You accuse me of skullduggery, without a proper investigation—" At my look, he gave up and shrugged. "All right! Yes, I ate them. You were clearing out old vegetables for the compost bin last night so I decided to help myself. I saved you time, really, by not asking you to make a snack for me."

"Right, tell it to the judge," I said, then laughed. "Well, I thank May's intuition. I really can use these tomatoes, Bran. But you," I turned back to Fancypants, "do not get to munch on these. They're for my beef marinara sauce for the spaghetti, so don't you touch them."

With a vaguely guilty look, Fancypants nodded. "I won't."

"All right then." I turned back to stir the garlic and onion. "Bran, thank May, will you? And are you coming to dinner with her to meet my great-grandmother?"

Bran hopped up on the counter next to me, dangling his legs over the side. "Do you want me to come? I'll be here, if you like."

I glanced up at him—even with him sitting on the counter, he was taller than I was. His eyes twinkled, and he had gathered his hair back in a manbun. He was handsome, as light as Faron was dark. Bran leaned down and brushed my cheek with a kiss.

"For luck," he whispered.

"Come to dinner," I said, though I still wasn't sure it was the best idea. "You'll end up meeting Grams at some point. It might as well be tonight."

"You need any help?" he asked. "Want me to dice anything for you?"

"No. Why don't you scram now? I'll see you later. Oh, and

34

would you tell May that my great-grandmother dresses for dinner. And she expects *us* to dress for dinner, as well. Also, another thank-you for all you've done around here. I sure appreciate it. Now, off with you."

As he slid off the counter and headed toward the door, I watched him retreat. He was a delicious-looking man. Though I wasn't ready to jump back into the sexual band-wagon yet, at least I had learned that it was okay to date again.

BY SEVEN, we were ready for dinner, but upon viewing the table, Grams informed me that no *proper* MacPherson set the table without proper placemats and napkins. So I dug through my linen closet until I found five placemats and four napkins. The napkins were bigger than Fancypants, so I found a small washcloth that would work for him and explained that he was to use it to wipe off his mouth when he was done eating.

The doorbell rang.

"Shall I watch the dinner while you greet our guests?" Grams asked.

I took off my apron. "Please. The bread is in the oven, wrapped in foil. If you could stir the sauce, I'll drain the spaghetti when I get back."

She took over as I hurried to answer the door.

I had changed into a dark green sundress that comple-mented my hair. Grams was wearing a circle skirt, belted over a pale blue satin blouse. I prayed she wouldn't drop any spaghetti on it, but then again, the woman was fastidious and I doubt if she'd ever spilled a drop of anything in her life.

May was wearing a camel-colored linen pantsuit that looked both breathable and yet chic, and Bran was wearing a pair of black slacks and a tidy polo shirt, with his hair slicked back into a manbun. He was carrying flowers, and May carried the pie she'd promised to make.

"I'm so glad you're here," I said. "Come in."

As I navigated an early evening discussion on manners with Grams, it had occurred to me that while we probably would have a great deal to talk about, any conversation with her was going to be fraught with me worrying about what I said or how I said it. I wondered if I'd ever feel relaxed around her—but she certainly made my relationship with my mother seem more comfortable than I had ever thought possible.

"Come in, please." I ushered them in, grateful to see them both. I herded them into the kitchen, to where Grams was still stirring the sauce.

"Grams, I'd like you to meet my neighbor, May Anderson, and her son, Bran. May and Bran, this is my great-grand-mother, Morgance MacPherson." I motioned for Grams to hand me the stirring spoon.

She moved over to greet May and Bran while I drained the noodles and poured them into a serving bowl, adding the sauce. I tossed the noodles and the sauce lightly, trying to avoid splattering myself. I set the spaghetti in the center of the table, next to the salad. Then I retrieved the bread from the oven, transferring the slices of the baguette to a tray.

Bran greeted Grams, then helped me by filling the goblets with merlot, while I filled the water glasses. Fancypants flew in and asked me to turn on the water so he could wash his hands—which was the cutest thing to watch—and then he took his place in the high chair. It might be originally made for babies, but it was perfect for dragonettes, too.

May stared at him, then cracked a smile. "Well, now I've seen everything. How on earth did you decide a high chair was going to work for a dragonette?"

"We made the fortuitous discovery at a rummage sale a couple weeks back when he landed in one and we realized that it gave him the perfect situation to eat from a plate at the table. I bought it and we polished it up."

Not only had I polished the metal parts, but I'd recovered the seat and back with a vinyl toile featuring dancing goats in black and white. From a distance, it looked shabby chic, rustic designer, but up close, it was easy to clean and functional.

I filled a bread-and-butter plate for him with spaghetti and a piece of bread but skipped the salad. Fancypants wasn't a vegetable connoisseur. I set the plate in front of him and he politely restrained himself from diving in before everyone else was seated. As I unfurled my napkin and placed it in my lap, I hoped that Grams wouldn't complain about the simple dinner, but she surprised me.

"This smells absolutely amazing," she said. "I seldom make pasta, but we eat a lot of potatoes, and I make a minced potato pie that I think you would enjoy."

I smiled. "I love pasta. It's comfort food. Say, Grams, who's watching your house while you live here?"

"Your aunt Diedre. She sends her love."

My paternal grandmother was dead, but Father's sister had stayed in Scotland, and she had never been to the US, even for his funeral. Diedre had moved in with Grams once Grandma died, having never married or moved out on her own.

"Grams, why hasn't Diedre ever lived away from home?" I knew as little about my aunt as I did my father.

Grams hesitated. "I don't want to make your guests uncomfortable," she said. "Some family secrets can be difficult to hear—"

"Don't mind us," May said. "We aren't here to judge

anyone. If it's private, maybe you'd better wait until you're alone with your great-grandmother to ask, Elphyra."

Grams stared at May for a moment, then shook her head. "I trust you. I'm extremely good at sizing up people, and I haven't been around for over a hundred years without learning how—and who—to trust." She turned to me. "Your aunt Diedre has a different father than your father did. She's part succubus."

And just like that, she opened a can of worms.

CHAPTER FOUR

THE SILENCE AFTER HER REVELATION WAS DEAFENING. I stared at Grams. May stared at Grams. Bran sat in startled silence, but he—too—stared at Grams. Fancypants was the only one not paying attention. His face was deep in his plate of spaghetti.

"My *aunt* is part succubus? You mean Grandma—"

"It's a bit of a story."

I glanced at May. "We have time," she told me.

"Very well. You know your grandfather died relatively young, correct?"

I thought back to the stories my mother had told me. "I don't know how young, since my father died when I was five. This isn't some family curse, is it? On the men? And I thought my grandparents immigrated here. Though, I guess it seems strange now how I never met them, if they lived in the States."

"They did immigrate to America. Your father was born here—he had dual citizenship. But after your grandfather died, your grandmother wanted to move back to Scotland. Malcolm was twelve when your grandpa died."

"So, Dad went back to Scotland with his mother but came back later to the States?"

"Yes. Your grandfather died here, you know. He loved his family—your grandmother was the only woman he gave his heart to. He adored your father, too, but he lived too easily. He thought he was invincible. He'd never had to face his mortality—no near misses, no debilitating diseases."

"I wish I could still look at the world through rose-colored glasses," I muttered.

"Yes, well, unfortunately, they can make you miss things that are necessary to sustain life. You may have traumatic memories from your attack, but it made you aware of how tenuous life can be, and how precious it is," Grams said.

Though I didn't want to admit it, I couldn't argue with her. "Well, you're right about that. So, what happened to Grandpa?"

"Terrance stopped in at a tavern one night for a pint. One pint became two, then three. Instead of calling for a taxi, my son decided to drive home. He swerved over the line and crashed into the car in the other lane. Both he and the other driver were killed."

I gasped. "Grandpa killed somebody driving drunk?" That was far worse than cancer, or any other sort of disease. He had destroyed somebody else's life along with his own.

Grams nodded. "Unfortunately, yes. A young man with a family. Your great-grandfather and I came over to attend your grandfather's funeral. We quietly paid blood money to the widow. She had three young children. It was Terrance's fault and our family never shirks its responsibilities. The money couldn't make up for the loss of the man, but it at least made it easier on his widow and children."

I sighed. I had a grudge against drunk drivers—Bree's brother had been killed by a drunk. He'd been crossing in the crosswalk one December evening when a driver swerved around the corner, making a left turn against the red light, and mowed Jeffrey down. The driver had gotten off with a hand slap—three years in exchange for wiping out a life—but at least he had paid a hefty price. His name had been expunged from the rolls of the Kalaloch Puma Pride, and his parents and his wife had paid blood money to Bree's parents since Jeffrey wasn't married. But Grams was right—no amount of money could make up for the loss of their loved one. Every year during the holidays, Bree's family felt the loss.

"What happened to Grandma?" I asked.

"Your grandmother struggled on. She had your father to think about. Malcolm was twelve when Terrance died. He became withdrawn. Going to school was hard on him because the children of the dead man went to the same school and he was ostracized. Sins of the parents, and so on. So Peter—your great-grandfather—and I packed the children up and took them back to Scotland. Elisa didn't want to move back to Stromness—where I live. Peter and I wanted them to stay near us, but Elisa said that she needed to make a fresh start. So, we helped her find a new home in Glasgow."

"Where does Aunt Diedre come in?"

"In 1979, a year after Terrance died, your grandmother started dating a man she met in a local pub. She didn't realize it at the time, but he was an incubus. They're rare, and seldom present themselves as who they really are. She fell for him and got pregnant. He vanished the day after she told him." Grams sighed. "I urged her to apply for an abortion, but she refused. She stubbornly believed that Karn would return for her. I'm convinced he put her under a glamour and he never bothered to remove it before he left."

"When did she find out that Karn was an incubus?"

"Not till Diedre was born. The doctor, a specialist with Otherkin, recognized something different about her and they put her through a battery of tests. Turned out, she had succubus blood in her. She doesn't have the full powers or personality, but the mix of witchblood and demon created an unstable mix. Diedre's always been clingy and afraid to go out into the world. Elisa ended up homeschooling her because, from her first year in school, Diedre was in and out of one fight after another." Grams wound spaghetti around her fork. "Diedre moved in with me when Elisa died, and I've kept an eye on her and helped her navigate life. So that's your aunt's story."

I wasn't sure what to think. Having an aunt who was part succubus sounded like it could be fun, but Grams gave me a long look, and I realized that maybe I shouldn't be so hasty.

"How does she handle being on her own now that you're gone?"

"I've hired a good friend to check in on her every day. They get along, and Muriel is trustworthy. Diedre will listen to her."

May cleared her throat. "That must have been rough for both your daughter and your granddaughter."

"It was," Grams said. "Malcolm had vowed to return to the United States, and the moment he turned eighteen, he took what little inheritance his father had willed to him and left home. He moved to the States and immediately met your mother," she added, turning to me.

"Mom said they fell in love at first sight. She was sixteen, and Grandma Anna wouldn't let her get married until she turned eighteen. Dad waited for her, and on the day of her eighteenth birthday, they got married. I came along two years later, in 1990."

Grandma Anna and Grandpa James were still alive, but they lived all the way across the country and I seldom saw them. They emailed now and then, but they were busy with their social circle and they traveled all over the world.

Grams turned to May. "I'm afraid we're leaving you out of the conversation."

"You have a fascinating family history. I'm not bored. I've never had the chance to meet an incubus or a succubus. How did your grandson—Elphyra's father—adapt to having a succubus for a sister?" May asked.

Grams smiled. "Malcolm loved his sister. He was so good with her. Even after he moved over to the States, he always kept in touch with her. He wrote her letters and called her every week. Diedre adored him. She's only ten years older than Elphyra."

"Yeah, but we've never had a chance to meet," I said. "Do you think she'll ever come to visit?"

Grams shook her head, helping herself to more spaghetti. "Honestly? No, I don't. She's agoraphobic, dear. As I said, I took her in when Elisa died. It was a nasty accident, her death was."

"How did she die? If it doesn't hurt too much to talk about it."

"Oh, I loved Elisa—she was a good daughter-in-law. But my son's actions broke her. She did her best to work through the pain, but she never could forgive him for what he did to, not only their family, but the victim's family. She was so conflicted. She went out for a walk and slipped off a cliff, falling to her death on the rocks below."

I wasn't sure how to ask, but Grams finished my thought for me.

"We were never sure if it was an accident, or deliberate. Diedre was fifteen when Elisa died. I took her in and she's lived with me since then. Peter had died the year before—he was 121, and he ended up with MWD."

"What's that?" I asked.

"Magical wasting disease. It happens when the magical energy becomes so thin that the body begins to draw on the life force. It's a rare disease, and it seems to be random. There's a genetic component, but it's a mutation, not hereditary." Grams shrugged. "It was hard, losing him. Peter and I didn't have a great romance, but we had a solid marriage and we loved each other. So, the year after he died, Diedre moved in."

"Do you get along with her?"

"As best as I can. I love her and she's no real trouble. But she's always felt like an outsider. I did my best to make her feel part of the family, but she's never expressed interest in meeting anybody else. The only person she ever loved—truly loved—was your father. She idolized her brother and when he died, she shut down. Oh, she eats and takes care of the house, and putters in the garden, but she never rebounded. She's content to watch over the garden and take care of the house, and I decided that it's best to just let her live in what comfort she finds."

"That's a lot," I said, taking a deep breath. "I'll need some time to process it." My mother had told me none of this.

"Take all the time you need," Grams said.

Nodding, I glanced over at Fancypants. His plate was empty and I needed something concrete to focus on. "You need more to eat?"

He lit up, licking his lips. Well, what passed for lips on a dragonette. He'd finished everything I'd served him.

"You want some more?"

"Thank you. Yes, please, if you would. More spaghetti."

Grams chuckled. "You are the cutest little thing. You are so polite—"

"Well, there really isn't a better way to be, is there?" Fancypants puffed up, looking proud as a peacock.

"True. Manners are vital to holding society together." Grams turned to Bran as I loaded up the dragonette's plate again.

"So, tell me, young man. Do you have a girlfriend?"

I froze. This was awkward. But then, Gran had that imperiousness that age often brought to the strong. She wasn't used to being contradicted or questioned, and she had a natural leadership that made people jump.

Bran cleared his throat. "Not exactly."

I let out my breath. While I liked Bran, I also liked Faron and I had no intention of taking on the label of "girlfriend" for either one at this point.

Grams glanced at me. "My granddaughter needs to step into life again." She paused, and I could feel her gaze boring a hole in my skull. "You two have dated, correct?"

"Grams, *stop*—" I said, a warning tone in my voice.

But Bran wasn't used to fending her off. "Yes, ma'am."

May laughed. "You aren't going to pull anything over on her, so you'd both better get used to it. Yes, Bran and Elphyra have been on a few dates, but they aren't exclusive. And there's nothing wrong with that. While I'd love to see them together, I realize it takes time and it's not my place to rush things."

And just like that, May managed to make my great-grandmother back off.

Grams paused, glancing at Bran and then at me. "I'll keep my silence, but I'm happy to hear you've noticed each other."

I decided to change the subject. Even though I'd talked to May and Bran about it already, Bree's problem seemed to be a good topic. "I was wondering. I promised Bree I'd go look at the graveyard next to her house. Some odd things have been happening over there. I thought I'd go tomorrow night—anybody want to go with me?"

"I can go with you," Bran said.

"I'm afraid my quilting club meets tomorrow evening," May said.

I turned to Grams. "What about you? You want to go with Bran and me?"

Grams gave me a smile. "I can do that. Now, May, tell me about your home. Elphyra says you are her nearest neighbor?"

As May began to talk about Brambleberry Farm, I went back to my dinner. But my thoughts weren't on Bran, or May or even Grams. They were on my cousin Diedre, and what she was facing. I wondered what other skeletons were hidden in the family closet, and how many of our relatives knew about her. I had a hundred questions, but I decided to wait until later to ask. We finished up the evening and May and Bran headed for home after setting a time for Bran and Grams to accompany me to the graveyard next to Bree's.

CHAPTER FIVE

THE NEXT MORNING, I SHOWED GRAMS AROUND STARLIGHT Hollow before I had to go back and open my shop. Fancy-pants opted to stay home—he was hooked on a morning show about antiques and so I turned on the TV, set the remote pointed at the television so he could press the buttons, and then Grams and I headed out.

We began our tour of the town starting with breakfast at Honey Badger's—a diner run by one of the local drag queens. By day, Honey was a metrosexual, smooth-as-silk gay man, but three times a week, he turned into Honey Badger, a trash-talking fine-as-wine drag queen who held a show at the Empire, a local underground nightclub for those who liked life on the edge.

While the majority of locals didn't attend, they all knew Honey and loved him with a passion usually reserved for their favorite pastor. Honey had acquired the unofficial title of Saint Honey, patron of the hungry. He donated all his profits from his drag shows to the local food bank. Since most everyone in town had—at one time or another—needed a little help, Honey was known as a benevolent benefactor. He also opened his diner one night a week as a soup kitchen, and kept the food he didn't sell during the day for the poor kids to stop by and take home to their hungry families.

I told Grams the story as we parked in the lot and crowded in for breakfast. We were lucky—a booth had opened—but, as usual, the place was packed. The food was good, the atmosphere over-the-top, and above all, eating at Honey's diner felt *fun*.

The walls were covered with pictures of all the old glamour girls—Marilyn and Jane, Bette and Joan, Greta and Heddy—you name it, Honey had pictures of them. My mother loved old movies and I'd grown up on them.

As we took our seats, sliding into the neon pink faux leather seats, Grams looked around and smiled. "Whoever runs this knows what they're doing. A simple step through the door and I'm smiling."

I was about to say she was right when Honey himself showed up. He was wearing a pair of black leggings, a long rainbow print tunic over the top, and his long blond hair was pulled back in a tight bun. Honey was trim and fastidious.

"Elphyra, hon, hello! It's been a while since I've seen you up this early." He handed us both menus, then stopped, staring at Grams for a moment. "Pardon me for being nosy, but do I detect a resemblance between the two of you?"

Grams and I shared the family nose—smooth and Roman—and we also shared a similar facial structure. Honey wasn't wrong. The resemblance was there if you chose to look for it.

"Honey, this is my great-grandmother, Morgance MacPherson. She's moving to the States from Scotland. She'll be living in Port Townsend. Grams, I'd like you to meet Honey. He owns the restaurant. My father was her grandson." I had no idea what Grams would say or do—I still didn't know her well enough to gauge whether she was socially tolerant, but I figured I'd find out in the next few moments.

Grams gracefully extended her hand. "Pleased to meet you, Honey. I love your diner—the atmosphere is charming."

Honey took Grams's hand and elegantly leaned over, planting a kiss on the top of it. "Ms. MacPherson, I am charmed to meet you. Your granddaughter has made a good home for herself here. I hope you enjoy your move to our country, and your visit to Starlight Hollow." He pointed to the menu. "Now, figure out what you'd like. Do you want coffee to start with?"

"I'll have a triple-shot vanilla latte, please. Iced," I said.

"Of course you will," Honey said. "Girl, you know all that caffeine can't be good for you." He tapped the order pad with his pencil.

"My granddaughter thrives on it," Grams said, a twinkle in her eye. "As for me, I'll start out with English breakfast tea."

"Tea's no better," Honey said, arching his eyebrows. "All right, coffee and tea coming up. Do you want a few minutes before ordering?"

"Yes, and you can stop the running commentary every time I order." I scowled, but then my expression slid. I couldn't keep a straight face. Not with Honey.

"Now, girl, since I don't hold breakfast shows, how else would I entertain you?" Honey wrinkled his nose, then bounced off with a grin.

After he left, Grams said, "He has more energy than all his customers combined. I'd like to catch one of his shows, if we can."

"I'm sure you'll have the chance to. Even if we can't see one while you're here, once you're settled in your new home, you can come down for a weekend and we'll go." I paused, then asked, "So, how does my mother feel about you moving here?" I thought I knew the real answer, but wanted to see what Grams had to say.

"Your mother is as enthusiastic about me moving into her

town as a canary watching the cat sit outside its cage. She also needs help, my dear." Grams shook her head. "When I say she isn't strong, I'm not trying to criticize her. But it's true. She was cushioned from the outer world for a long time. Malcolm used to write to me. By the time he met Catharine, his mother was focused on Diedre. She didn't have time for him."

"He and Mom loved each other a lot, didn't they?"

"Yes. As I said last night, they met in high school. It was love at first sight. I knew it—I could tell from his letters. I took it upon myself to check out her family background. What I learned was that they were a fine, upstanding family who shielded their children from the problems of life as long as they could."

"My mother never learned how to cope with stress?"

"She never had to face problems. I thought Malcom's death would finish her."

I thought back to my childhood. Everything was fine till my father died. And then... "You're right. When my father died, I had to toughen up. I often felt like I was the mother and she was the child. I did everything I could to avoid worrying her or making her upset." My mother had lived in a perpetual fog of sorrow for a long time.

"Aye, she handed the responsibilities of an adult over to you when you were far too young. I can't forgive her for that, but she had no coping mechanisms."

"I love her, regardless. I don't always like her, but I love her. I'm glad Aunt Ciara lives nearby—that helps."

Grams smiled. "I love your mother, too. We don't always agree, but I think she was good for your father. He was as headstrong as Terrance was."

"How did my father die? Nobody ever told me. My mother won't talk about him, and nobody ever came out and told me what happened. I tried looking it up—I checked the records for his obituary, but no reason for death was given."

Grams started to speak, but then held her tongue as Honey brought our drinks.

"Now, what can I get you?"

"I'll have the waffle with berries, and three sides of bacon, along with a side of sausage."

Honey turned to Grams. "And for you?"

"Oatmeal, with brown sugar and raisins. I'll also have a ham steak on the side." Grams handed him her menu and we waited for him to leave. After he had headed back into the kitchen, she leaned across the table and took my hands. "Are you sure you want to know?"

"I hate not knowing. My mother hinted he was sick, but I have no idea if that was true."

"Your father had too many pressures on his shoulders, my dear. He was well off, but his business partners weren't happy with him."

I realized that I didn't know what my father's profession had been. "What did he do?"

"He was on the Witches' Council for Port Townsend, high up the ranks. I'm not sure what went down—I was in Scotland, remember—but one night, he was found dead in his office with no apparent cause. The Witches' Council hushed it up, but there were conflicting reports as to whether he committed suicide or whether he was murdered, possibly by magic." Grams's eyes grew dark, and she pursed her lips together when she finished speaking. I had the impression she was trying to avoid crying.

"Mom saw the Washing Woman recently," I said.

"I know. She told me. We'll just have to wait and see what happens."

Honey brought our food, and I settled back in my seat. Grams was done talking about it, I could tell. I turned the topic toward my shop and Grams followed suit. But in the back of my mind, I wondered: did my mother know anything about this? And why hadn't she told me about it? And did my father kill himself, or was he murdered?

AFTER WE FINISHED BREAKFAST, I asked Honey when his next show was going to be, and then Gran and I headed out into the town. It was nine, so we had time to poke around. I'd left a note on my shop door that I would be opening an hour late, which gave us nearly two hours to explore downtown Starlight Hollow.

As we strolled along the main drag, I did my best to ignore thoughts about my father and his death. "Over there's one of the best bakeries in town—Marline's Sweetshop. And next to it is a vintage shop that always has something gorgeous on the racks."

"Let's go take a look," Grams said.

We waited until traffic had cleared—which took all of five minutes—and then crossed the street. While Starlight Hollow had a rush hour of sorts, it didn't last long. And traffic the rest of the day was scattered, ever present in a slow trickle.

As we entered Vintage Romance, my phone rang. It was Faron. I tapped Grams on the shoulder. "I'm going to step outside and take this," I said, pointing to the "No cellphone use" sign.

"All right. I'll poke around until you're done," she said, disappearing down one of the aisles.

I popped back outside and answered. "Hey, what's up?"

"Have you thought more about introducing me to your great-grandmother?" Faron didn't bother with a hello.

"Well, hello to you, too. What is this fixation you have

with meeting Grams?" I couldn't understand his enthusiasm. It wasn't like we were exclusive. It wasn't time to "meet the parents."

"I want to see what she's like," he said. "Anyway, what I really called about was to suggest dinner Friday night—just us." His voice curled around me, making me shiver. He had one of those voices that conjured up cold wintery nights under the stars, watching the aurora shimmer across the sky.

I hesitated, then figured that Grams wouldn't mind an evening or two alone. I could invite May over if she wanted company. "All right. Friday night, seven o'clock?"

"See you then," he said. "And wear that red dress. The one I saw in your closet the other day." Faron had helped me drag a heavy box off the top shelf of my closet a few days back. I hadn't realized he had been eyeing my wardrobe while he'd been at it.

I knew exactly what dress he was talking about but decided to play with him a bit. "You mean that long maxi dress? The one that looks like it's out of the Woodstock generation?"

He snorted. His voice low, he said, "You *know* the one I'm talking about. I want to see you in it. Your ass would look so good in that."

My ass, in fact, looked great in that dress. So did my boobs. It was a wiggle dress, off-the shoulder and formfitting to every curve. Ruched all the way down, the material showed every curve, and came to high thigh level. The fact that Faron wanted me to wear it set my heart beating. He wanted me— that had been obvious on our first date, but I'd kept him at arm's length. Not because I didn't want him, but because I was overwhelmed by my feelings.

"You want to see me in that?" I asked, my breath catching in my chest.

"What do you think?" Faron asked. "I can picture you in it—and trust me, I'm picturing you in that dress right now."

I forced myself to calm down so my voice wouldn't tremble. "All right. I'll wear it. But you'd better take me to somewhere I can show it off." As Faron laughed, I added, "And I'm not talking your bedroom."

"Killjoy," he said, but chuckled. "I'll see you Friday night at seven. I'll pick you up. No arguments."

As I slid my phone in my pocket, I shivered. Every time I got near Faron Collinsworth, my body reacted. It was getting harder and harder to put him off. But was I ready to start sleeping around again?

AFTER VISITING VINTAGE ROMANCE, I showed Grams a high-end lingerie boutique where I'd taken to buying my underwear, then we stopped in at an art store since Grams liked to paint, where we bought her some watercolor paper, paints, an easel, and the other supplies she needed to set up her own little artist's studio.

"I can leave them here for when I come visit." She insisted on carrying the bags herself.

"Grams, do you mind if I go out Friday night?" We were heading back to my car.

"On a date, you mean?"

"Right."

"I don't mind, on one condition. I want to meet the mystery man. Unless it's Bran, in which case I've met him and highly approve." She glanced at me as a car swept past, a little close to the sidewalk for comfort. "What aren't you telling me?"

I sighed. "You're not going to let this drop, are you?"

"No, so you might as well tell me now," she said.

I took a deep breath. "Grams, you might as well know that I'm dating both Bran Anderson, and Faron Collinsworth, the King of the Olympic Wolf Pack."

With that, I opened the door to the car and slid in, not waiting for her to answer.

BY THE TIME we reached the bay, Grams had quit ranting. Well, to be fair, she hadn't ranted. She'd pointed out all the reasons why wolf shifters and witches didn't see eye-to-eye.

"I don't care if history left us on opposite sides," I said. "To be honest, when I first met Faron, I didn't like him either. In fact, we had a few run-ins that could have left us enemies, if we hadn't...if he hadn't..." I wasn't sure to tell her that he'd come asking for my advice on a magical matter, and that I'd helped him. Like most witches, Grams had a heightened disregard for wolf shifters.

"The wolf shifters left us to die at the hands of the Inquisitors. They turned us over to them to save their own skins," Grams said. "They were as bad as the warlocks."

"But it's not like that anymore," I argued. "The Inquisitors don't exist anymore and the churches have faded in their power to tyrannize people. They work *with* us now, not against us. The warlocks have faded since there's no gain to turning us over for bounties. Granted, there are still hate groups, but they're on the fringe."

"What do you think his family would think?" Grams asked.

"He's the King. That doesn't matter. He can do what he wants," I muttered.

"Don't count on it. He may be King but if his mother and father are still alive, you are going to have a steep road to climb."

"They aren't alive, though he has a brother. It's not like I'm marrying him. We're just dating." I parked the car and turned off the engine. "Now, do you want to see the bay before I have to be back to open up the shop?" I opened the door and jumped out, unwilling to continue the argument.

Grams followed suit, and I had the feeling I'd temporarily won the battle. That didn't mean she wouldn't continue the argument, but for now, she allowed me to show her around the bay. We walked down the steps by the Grapevine—the nursery I bought my plants from—and sat on one of the driftwood logs, staring out into the water.

"It's beautiful. It reminds me of our shorelines," Grams said after a while. "So, you really like this wolf shifter?"

I snorted. "We butted heads several times before deciding to call a truce. And then...well...I don't know how *much* I like him, but enough to date, I guess. He has a good heart below that gruff exterior."

"Are you sure you aren't interested in Bran? You said you were dating him."

I could hear the last-ditch effort in her voice.

"Grams, I like *both* of them, but I have no plans on getting serious right now. I don't even know if I can sustain an emotional relationship right now. Rian may have put his seal of approval on me moving on—he came to me and told me I had to let go, that I need to do some sort of cord-cutting ceremony—but I don't think I'm ready to give my heart to anybody else. Not yet." I leaned my elbows on my knees and propped my chin on my hands.

Grams moved closer, putting her arm around me. "It was hell, wasn't it?"

Her tone of voice said she understood. I leaned my head on her shoulder.

"I can't forget, Grams. I don't think I'll ever be able to forget the things the Butcher did to Rian. And all I could do was sit and watch. I *know* it's not my fault. I know that I'm not the one to blame...but I'm here, and he's not, and he died to protect me."

"Then go out, date, keep it light, and time will tell you when you're ready," Grams said, kissing my forehead. She wrapped her arm around my shoulders and we sat, watching the waves crash against the shore.

CHAPTER SIX

I HAD A HECTIC DAY DEALING WITH CUSTOMERS—
including a couple of Karens. One had decided that she didn't
like the smell of her new candles, although she had smelled
them before she bought them. The other had wanted to
return a tarot reading because "It was right but I didn't like
that it happened." I wasted over an hour on them before
refunding their money and telling them both never to return.

By afternoon, I was counting the minutes till three when I
could close up shop. As soon as I turned the shop sign to
"Closed" and locked the door behind me, I breathed a
massive sigh and headed across the parking lot to the house.

"You finished?" Fancypants asked as I climbed the porch
steps and slumped onto the hanging swing I'd asked Bran to
install.

"I'm stick-a-fork-in-me done. I'm so done. Sometimes I
wonder why I decided to open a store, but I have to do something and I don't want to work nine-to-five for someone else.
I guess every store encounters a few bad apples."

Fancypants fluttered around me, finally landing on the top

of my head. He coiled his neck down so he was staring at me, albeit from an upside-down perspective. "How are things going with your great-grandmother?"

"Better than I'd expected. I have a feeling that the other shoe has yet to drop, though. She said she moved over to make sure my magic doesn't go awry from the trauma I went through, but I have a feeling it's more than that. I'll wait to find out, because if I just come out and ask her, she won't tell me." I glanced at my phone. "It's almost time for dinner. We're eating early before we head to Bree's. I'd better call her to make sure she still wants us to come over."

The phone rang once before Bree answered. She sounded breathless. "Hey! Are you still planning to come over tonight?"

"Yes, and Bran and Grams are coming with me. Why, is something wrong?"

"I feel like I'm going a little crazy. The feeling of being watched has increased. This morning when I was taking a shower, I felt creeped out, like I was being watched. This is ridiculous. If it's a ghost, well, I haven't seen any sign of activity. I really appreciate you coming over. I'll see you in a bit."

After she hung up, I stared at my phone.

Bree wasn't given to making up things or exaggerating. I tucked my phone away and headed in to make dinner for Grams and me.

THAT EVENING, when Bran arrived, he, Grams, and I headed to the graveyard next to Bree's property, after I texted her to tell her that we were on the way.

"So, this Bree. She's your best friend?" Grams asked.

"Bree and I are like sisters," I said. "Though we don't

often fight. She's a puma shifter. We've known each other since high school, and I love her to pieces. She owns an outdoor expedition company, and takes groups of hikers on tours around the area."

Grams raised her eyebrows. "Does she have any suggestions for easy walking tours for those of us a wee bit along in age?"

I snorted. I had the feeling Grams could outwalk me any day. "You took walks every day at home, didn't you?"

"Oh, I can walk for miles, if the ground is even enough. When I was young, I'd hike through the highlands every summer with my friends. We'd go out and work magic in the open areas, and more than once we were chased by kelpies. The will-o'-the-wisps tried to entrap us. It's a wonder we came out of some of those encounters alive," she added, laughing.

"Weren't you afraid?" I asked. I never worried when I was young, never afraid. But now, fear dogged my heels.

"Not really. We knew we were taking risks, but we also knew that we were out there together, and it's always harder to take on a group rather than an individual." She glanced at me, studying my face. "We should have been more cautious, though. Taking a risk is one thing, but being foolhardy is asking for trouble."

"I wish I wasn't as afraid as I am. I never used to be, but after Rian, it's like the fear's become a ball and chain. I drag it everywhere, and I don't know how to get rid of it. Although May helped break the connection between the Butcher and me, and he can't find me just by thinking about me, I find myself fretting about things I never used to worry about. I worry about my friends, too."

"Do you think the fear has become a habit?" Bran asked.

I shrugged. "I don't know. I guess so. I'm still dealing with so many issues surrounding his death that I can barely see through the mire. He came to me in spirit, but the guilt isn't something you can just drop when you feel like it. I've had therapy and I've made a lot of progress, but I still feel knotted by anxiety at times." I paused as we came to the foot of the porch steps, where Bree joined us, after locking the dogs in the house. "Bree, this is my great-grandmother, Morgance. Grams, this is Bree, my best friend."

Bree was waiting on her porch. She held out her hand. "Welcome to my home, and to the US. What would you like me to call you?"

"There's no need to stand on ceremony. Since you're Elphyra's best friend, why don't you call me 'Grams,' like she does? If that makes you uncomfortable, feel free to call me Morgance." Grams shook Bree's hand. "I was telling my great-granddaughter that I might ask you about day trips with an easy hiking trail. I'd love to see the area by foot."

"Sure, we can do that," Bree said. She turned to me. "Are you going out to the graveyard, then? I'm still spooked."

"Walk us to the gate, and you can wait there. We'll be fine." I motioned for the others to follow me and we headed toward the gate that divided Bree's property from the graveyard. "Hopefully, the fact that we're in a group will prevent the serial killer from coming after us."

"Serial killer?" Grams asked.

"Yeah, we have a serial killer in Starlight Hollow right now," Bree said. "Nobody's been able to pin him down. The cops think he's a wolf shifter, and so far, he's killed...what... five victims?"

"And he's left no trace of who he is?" Grams asked.

"No." I shrugged. "I've talked to one of the ghosts and was able to verify that the murderer is definitely a shifter of some sort."

"You said a wolf shifter?" Grams gave me a sideways look.

"Daisy Parker—the sheriff—has checked out Faron's Pack. That's how Faron and I began talking. He wanted me to help exonerate one of his lieutenants, who was under suspicion. He *was* exonerated, but they haven't found the killer yet."

"What did Faron want you to do? You're not an officer of the law."

"No, but he asked me to help by talking to the ghosts of the deceased. While that didn't provide the name of the murderer, at least the shifter under suspicion was able to provide an airtight alibi for the third—I think it was—killing. They're the main Pack in the area, so unless someone in the Pack is harboring a deep secret, it can't be one of them." I frowned. I didn't for a second believe that anyone in Faron's Pack was to blame. In the time I'd gotten to know him better, I came to understand how strong of an honor code he embraced for his Pack.

"Do you think there might be a rogue running around?" Grams asked.

I shrugged. "Maybe. I don't know much about shifter society, except what I've learned from him. Anyway, Daisy calls me out to talk to ghosts now and then, but she said to otherwise keep out of this case. She doesn't want me to end up dead like the others."

"Very good advice," Bran said.

Grams pointed to the graveyard. We were at the gate now. "There are old spirits there, in that cemetery."

"That isn't surprising. It was established in 1865, I believe. There hasn't been a new occupant for seventy-some years. And yes, there are ghosts in there, but my instincts tell me that whatever is watching Bree isn't a spirit. Maybe a demon or some other astral creature, but the spirits there seemed oblivious to the living, as far as I can tell."

I stepped through the gate and held it open for the others. Bree stayed at the gate, on her side of the lawn, as Bran, Grams, and I crossed into the cemetery. Once again, I was overwhelmed by a feeling that something wasn't right.

I turned to Grams. "What do you think?"

"You're right—not a spirit," she said. "The spirits here are so old they're nearly memories. They're oblivious, for the most part. But I *do* feel what you were talking about—it's an invasive presence. Male, I think. And I honestly don't think that he's from the outer planes." Grams looked around, then walked over to one of the trees.

The graveyard was small—only about two acres. Yew trees were scattered throughout the grounds, as were a couple of mausoleums. Yew was the wood of the dead, of the underworld. The grass between the headstones was knee-deep and ivy had begun to wind its way around some of the stones. I had no idea when the lawn had last been mowed.

In the center of the cemetery stood a large fountain that had long gone dry. Gothic in nature, a grim reaper tenderly held the skeleton of a baby, and it looked as if the water had poured out from the scythe. I leaned against the base, but the only chill I felt was from the marble cooling from the day.

Grams poked around the yew tree nearest the gate. "Come here, please."

I headed over, with Bran following. "What did you find?"

"I don't know, but this is the center of the disruption." She stood back and crossed her arms, tapping her index finger against her left elbow. She eyed the tree as though she might be getting ready to cross-examine it. "Check the hollows."

Bran and I peeked into the notches caused by the burls and whorls of the trees. If we were in Eastern Washington, I'd use a stick, rather than poke my hand in a dark hole. Over there, they had rattlers and black widows. But here, there

were few venomous creatures, so while we might find a spider
or a bug or a garter snake, bites seldom resulted in much
beyond a mild discomfort.

Bran paused, his hand inside one of the holes near the
crotch where a big branch met the trunk of the tree. "I feel
something."

"What is it?"

He withdrew his hand, holding a cord. "Where the hell
does this lead? It's pinned to the trunk. Here, move so I can
climb up."

I stood back as he took hold of the branch overhead and
swung himself up like a gymnast. He was built, all right, and
he moved lithely. It was becoming harder to avoid thoughts
of what he looked like naked, and what he might be like in
bed. But the next moment, all thoughts of sex vanished as he
pulled the cord away from the tree.

"What did you find?" I asked.

"It's a battery pack that was in the hole and the cord
attached to it leads...well, I'll be damned. Look at this." He
reached into a V in the branch that was directly facing Bree's
house. "It's a camera, like a webcam, kind of."

"A surveillance camera?"

"Yeah. And..." he held the camera up to his eye, leaning as
close as he could to the original position in which he had
found it. "It's pointed toward her bedroom and it's got a
powerful zoom lens. I can see her bed from here."

"Crap," I said. "Bring it down here."

He dropped out of the tree, holding up the camera. "Well,
I think I can definitively say that this wasn't put there by any
ghost. Whoever placed the camera knew exactly what he was
doing."

I turned back to Bree's house. "Where there's one, there
are bound to be more. Let's go check out her yard and
house."

As we headed back to the gate, I wondered how we were going to tell Bree that some pervert had been watching her, and—if we were right—had most likely installed other surveillance gadgets around her house. Somehow, *creepy human* blew *irritated ghost* right out of the water.

CHAPTER SEVEN

BREE WAS WAITING FOR US, AN EXPECTANT LOOK ON HER face. She glanced at us, her expression suddenly giving way to worry. "You found something, didn't you?"

"Yes, we did," I said. "It's not what you think, either. In fact, I hate to tell you this, but it's worse than a ghost." I draped my arm around her waist. "Come on, let's take a walk over to the picnic table." Just in case anybody had bugged her house, I didn't want them to know we had found them out. That would come soon enough as it was.

Looking confused, she let us walk her over to the picnic table that was sitting in the middle of her front yard. The evening was cooling off. It was probably in the mid-sixties, though still pleasant. Overhead, the sky showed the first sprinkle of stars amidst that twilight silver, streaked with poofs of white clouds. Birdsong echoed through the air, reverberating through the evening, and the crickets chirped away on nature's version of *The Dating Game*. The scent of warm grass and dusty air laden with pollen hung heavy around us. It would have been the perfect time for a late picnic.

"What did you find?" Bree asked. Her voice was shaking—

our nervousness had rubbed off onto her. "Was there anything out there? You said it's worse than a ghost? Is it a demon?"

"No demon. You sensed something, all right—but whoever they are, they aren't dead. Bran, show her what you found." I motioned for him to set the camera on the table.

Her eyes widened as he did. "What the hell?"

"The camera's super sensitive, and it was set on zoom to the point of where he could see directly into your bedroom. He...well, I suppose it *could* be a woman, but we sensed masculine energy. Anyway, we want to check through the house for any other cameras or surveillance items." Bran shrugged. "I'd say you have a stalker."

Bree paled. "Crap. You're right—this is worse than a ghost. Who the fuck has been watching me?"

"That's the million-dollar question," Grams said. "Do you have any disgruntled ex-boyfriends? Girlfriends?"

After a moment, Bree shook her head. "I don't date often, and most of the guys I used to date are married now. I can't think of anybody who was so upset when we broke up that he'd want to stalk me."

With a glance around us, Grams said, "We should go through the house before whoever it is realizes that we've found their camera. Once we're inside, say nothing. We don't know that there isn't some sort of bug inside, as well."

"I don't have a bug scanner," Bran said. "How do we find one if there is?"

I called Daisy. "Hey, this is Elphyra. Do you have anything that can scan for listening devices?" I quickly outlined what had happened. "We're thinking that if somebody set up surveillance on her from the graveyard, then there's a good chance they've been inside her house somehow and have installed bugs."

"That's troublesome. Bree should file a report with us.

And yes, actually. I *do* have a couple handheld bug zappers. Not only do they find bugs, but they also can fry them. I'm about to head out for a meeting. Would you like me to drop them off? It's on my way." She sounded out of breath, as though I had caught her on the run.

"That would be great. We'll talk to you in a few." And with that, we went back to the table and waited.

Daisy showed up ten minutes later. We were still waiting outside. She pressed the bug zapper in my hand and quickly showed me how to use it. "The light turns green when you're within a foot of a listening device. If you press the yellow button—that one right there—it will fry the bug. Or you can smash it, if you like—once you find it."

"Can you take a report?" I asked.

"I'm on my way to a meeting," Daisy said. "I can't stay, but I'll drop back in about forty-five minutes and I can take a report then. I'd send a man to help with the bug search, but honestly, we're so short-staffed right now that I'm afraid I can't spare anybody."

We thanked her. Daisy headed for her car, and the rest of us headed toward the house.

I was carrying the device, and—as we entered the house— I swept it around. Bree didn't have a landline so any bug couldn't be attached to the phone. The fact that she was a minimalist made the hunting easier. As we neared the kitchen, the handheld unit vibrated and I looked around. I was standing near a clock. I pointed to it and Bran lifted it off the hook from the wall. He turned it over and sure enough, there was what looked like a miniature motherboard attached to the back. It was attached to a miniature camera.

I pointed the detector toward it and pressed the yellow

button. There was an audible sizzle and the light on the camera went out. One down. How many to go?

Bree was visibly upset, but she kept quiet as we swept through the rest of her house. We found two more devices—one in the bathroom and the other in her bedroom. Both were connected to cameras. The one in the bathroom was aimed directly at the shower. The one in her bedroom was aimed at her bed from where it was tucked in the foliage of a dried wreath hanging on the wall.

After we had found and fried all bugs and cameras, we did a second sweep to make certain we hadn't missed anything.

I sat down at the kitchen table, shaking my head. "Well, I didn't expect that when we started into the graveyard. I know Grams already asked, but try—can you think of *anybody* who might be responsible for this?"

Bree shook her head. "As I said, I don't have any irate exes. I don't date often, and when I have, we've broken it off amicably."

"They don't have to be irate," Bran said. "Anybody who didn't want to break up? Was there anybody who wanted to date you but whom you refused? Any unrequited lovers?"

She sighed. "I get a lot of offers to date, but most of them are from tourists who are passing through. They've usually either taken one of my expeditions or are going to take one. I never date customers. It leads to trouble."

"That's a good policy," I said. "But have any of them ever gotten pushy?"

Bree thought back. "I don't think so. A couple guys were jerks about it, but that doesn't happen often."

"Would you mind if we have a cuppa while we wait?" Grams asked.

"Of course," Bree said.

"Let me." I put the kettle on. When I searched through her cupboard, all I came up with was a box of English breakfast tea. The rest of her drinks were various flavors of coffee. Like me, she preferred her caffeine American-style.

As I was heating the water, my phone dinged and I checked my messages. I had a new text from Faron, asking me to call him. I glanced at the back door.

"I'll be right back. Bran, would you watch the kettle?"

"Sure thing," he said.

Grams was busy talking with Bree, so I took the opportunity to slip onto the back porch. As soon as I'd closed it behind me, I called Faron.

"Hey, what's up?" I asked.

"I can't wait till Friday night. I wanted to hear your voice again," he said.

My heart skipped a beat and I smiled. "I'm over at Bree's. We're investigating the graveyard next to her house."

His voice took on a sudden gruffness. "Who's 'we'?"

The longer I knew Faron, the longer I had to admit that I'd been wrong about him. Oh, he'd been wrong about me too, but at least we weren't having a pissing contest in the snow any more. But he and Bran—there was no way they were ever going to be buddies.

"Grams is with me, and Bran came along too."

"Bran?"

I rushed ahead, not wanting to go down that road. "We found something disturbing."

Faron paused, then he said, "What did you find?"

I told him about the cameras and recording devices. "Somebody's stalking her, and we have to find out who."

Immediately, the jealousy vanished. "Crap. That's not good. If I can help, ask. That's no way to treat a woman."

"No, it's not." I paused, not wanting to insult him. "I have a question," I finally said. "I want to ask you something but it could be taken as rude so I'm going to preface it with this: I don't mean it in a rude way at all."

"Ask away," Faron said, laughing as he added, "At least I know you're not telling me to go eat my can of Alpo."

I blushed, groaning. As I said, I'd been as wrong about him as he had about me, and I'd gotten my own jabs in. "No, not at all. Um...do wolf shifters have a heightened sense of tracking ability? Like...for scents?"

He snorted. "You mean, are we good bloodhounds?"

"Something of that nature. In the wild, wolves hunt and track their prey."

"Why do you ask?"

"I was wondering if you could smell the tree trunk that was holding the camera. Maybe you can catch a scent? Maybe track the person down that way?"

"So, you want to know if I can track the stalker down?"

"Pretty much," I said. "It's not that I don't trust the cops, but they have their hands full with the serial killer, as well as every other idiot around town who decides to get in a bar brawl."

"I hate to disappoint you, but I doubt if I can do anything. I *can* take a look. There is a small chance that, when I'm in wolf form, I'll smell something. I have Bree's number. I'll text her tomorrow and give it a try. Chances are, whoever planted those devices did it some time ago. Smells dissipate quickly." He cleared his throat. "So, Friday night... Will I get to meet your great-grandmother then? Or am I being conveniently relegated to the closet, along with all your other skeletons?"

"I know it doesn't seem fair, but Faron, you know how you and I butted heads at first? Multiply that by a thousand. I told Grams we were dating. She didn't take it well." It wasn't like we were engaged. If we were, I would have 100 percent stood up for him. But it was easier to leave things quiet for now. "She didn't forbid me to see you, but she's not happy."

"I can change her mind," he said, then before I could

71

respond, added, "I'll talk to you later. I'll text Bree tomorrow." And the line went silent.

I stared at my phone for a moment, feeling vaguely guilty. But I didn't have the energy to soothe his ego, so I pocketed my phone and returned to the table, where we went back to our tea while waiting for Daisy.

AFTER DAISY FINISHED TALKING to Bree, she promised to have a patrol car make a couple passes by the house during the night.

Grams, Bran, and I headed back to my house. Bran headed for home, while Grams kissed me good night and retired to the guest room. I decided to spend some time with the stars and, once on the patio, I leaned back in the rocking chair, staring at the skies. A moment later, Fancypants joined me.

"Are you okay?" he asked, flying over to land on my shoulder.

"I don't know, to be honest. Grams...is both exactly what I expected and yet, nothing like I expected. I know that sounds contradictory, but..."

"Are you unhappy with her? You sound unhappy."

I gazed up at the spreading field of stars overhead. "No, not with *her*. To be honest, I'm unhappy with *me*. With how I behaved on the phone with Faron tonight. I feel like I'm pretending like he doesn't exist. I know I hurt his feelings. Yet, I don't want Grams tearing him to shreds." I searched my feelings. Was I being truthful with myself? Or was I lying to myself again? I searched my heart, but mostly I realized that I was tired. I was tired of grieving. I was tired of living in fear. I was tired of feeling guilty.

"You're at a crossroads, you know," Fancypants said. "You're being forced to make choices."

"I know, and that pisses me off. I want to be left in peace." But the words felt hollow. I would never be in peace—not again. I pulled my knees to my chest and wrapped my arms around them.

"Aren't you a little bit angry?" Fancypants asked.

I glanced at him. He'd flown from my shoulder to the arm of the bench. "What do you mean?"

"You always sidestep the mention of anger. You talk about guilt and fear, but I think you're angry at Rian for leaving you. You're angry he died, and you feel guilty over that anger."

I sat still, trying to ignore the rumblings that echoed in my heart. Fancypants was right, even though I didn't want to admit it. For over a year, I'd ignored the feelings because they made me feel guilty, and that in turn made me angrier. But the dam broke, and I glared at the dragonette, my words pouring out in an angry flood.

"*Of course* I'm angry he died!" I burst into tears. "*All right*, I'm angry at Rian. Are you happy now? He died and left me alone. I know he couldn't help it, and he was protecting me, but he died and I sat there, watching him die. I watched the blood drain out of him. I watched him have an orgasm as the Butcher killed him. I watched the rats come in to eat his body while I was forced to sit there, alone, unable to do anything. I watched everything happen, and I wasn't allowed to look away—"

At that moment, the front door opened and Grams came out, wearing a long robe over her nightgown. "Whatever's going on out here? What's the matter?"

She swooped in and sat near me, pulling me into her arms. "Tell me what happened."

"I…" I didn't know how to begin to explain, but I finally

73

choked out the words. "I've had these panic attacks ever since Rian died. I get so angry—"

"Survivor's guilt," Fancypants said.

"I've worked with a therapist," I said. "I've done all that, but I'm *still* angry. He died and left me here to deal with all of these memories. It's not rational, I know that. Even though he came to me and asked me to let go, it's so hard."

"Well, that's why we call it emotion. It's not logical. Few of our feelings and actions are, when you get down to it. But Elphyra, you're a MacPherson. And MacPhersons carry on."

"Isn't it dangerous to repress feelings?" I asked, hiccupping.

"To repress them? Yes. But controlling them is another matter. Have you held a cord cutting ceremony yet?"

"No," I said. "I haven't been able to."

"Then we will—because he asked you to let him go and you *must* honor his memory and wishes. It would also help to find a way to physically work through your feelings. Do you belong to a gym?" She took me by the shoulders, holding me steady.

I gulped back my tears. "I don't. No. There's one in town, but I haven't gone since I moved here." I closed my eyes, feeling the emotions swirling inside of me. "I'm afraid of my feelings. They're ugly and angry and they feel dangerous. I don't want them building up inside."

Grams shook her head. "Dry your eyes. You've cried enough. At some point, you must pick up the pieces and go on. Rian's dead, and it wasn't your fault. He died a tragic death, but women have watched their men walk into the shadow of death for eons, knowing that there was a good chance their beloveds wouldn't return, and yet they carried on. They had to."

"But how? *How* did they carry on?"

"They carried on by setting one foot in front of another.

They carried on because *that's what we do*. That's what *any* survivor does. You carry on. You mourn, you rail against the gods, then you move on, even when you don't feel ready. I mourned my husband's death, and I carried on. I mourned my son's death. It wasn't an honorable one, but I mourned him and let him go, and did my best to make up for his short-comings. I mourned my grandson's death, and I moved on."

I wiped my eyes. "You're one tough broad, Grams."

"You bet your ass I am. I'm not unsympathetic, but there's been far too much navel-gazing today for my tastes. The MacPherson clan guards the Highlands. And those of us with magical blood guard against the monsters that seek entrance to this world. That's the main reason I'm here—to help you understand the lineage you represent. It's time you learned about your heritage. Your mother knows some of it, but I think she tried to block it out when your father died. Unfortunately, with no clear indication of how he died, it made it worse for her."

"My mother calls me every week, like clockwork, to make sure I'm all right."

"It's good practice," Grams said. "But she's lived in limbo since your father passed. While I can't help her, I can keep you from doing the same."

I leaned forward, resting my arms on my knees as I stared at my fingers. Overhead the stars shimmered. Their light came to us from the distant past. That past still lived in our vision, but in reality, a number of those stars no longer existed.

"I know you're right," I whispered. "I know it's time to say goodbye. To let go and step fully into the life I have now."

"Are you afraid you'll be disrespecting Rian's memory?" Grams asked.

I thought about her question for a moment. "No. As I said, he came to me about six weeks ago and gave me permission to move on. In fact, he insisted. I just... Stepping through that door...isn't easy. It's easier to live in the known, even if the present is painful. Stepping into an uncertain future is terrifying."

"It can be," Grams said, leaning back. "But instead of staring down at the ground, at the past that's dead and buried, look up at the stars. *Yes*, some of them *are* dead. But what about all those stars who continue to thrive and live? What about all the experiences waiting for you to give them a platform, to give them actual life?" She paused, then added, "I can't force you to move on, but I can stop enabling you to continue hiding."

I thought for a moment, then let out one final sigh. "All right. I know when I'm fighting a losing battle. I don't want to be like my mother—mourning for decades. Because though I love her, she interferes with everybody and everything in a rush to avoid her own feelings. And I don't want to be that person." Resolved to put the past to rest, I stood. "Teach me what I need to know."

And Grams smiled, winking at me.

CHAPTER EIGHT

"Wake up! Grams is making breakfast." Fancypants flapped his wings in my face, and as I opened my eyes, squinting at him, he breathed out a puff of smoke.

Coughing, I forced myself to sit up. The light streamed through my bedroom window, unimpeded by any clouds. I yawned and stretched. "All right, I'm up. And when did you start calling her 'Grams'?"

"She suggested it this morning. She said that since you're her great-granddaughter, I'm her great-granddragonette. I'm honored. I think Grams would never offer someone the chance to call her that unless she liked them." Fancypants landed on the quilt rack, which was devoid of any quilt. I always planned to buy one, but I kept forgetting. Rian's mother had been going to make us one as a wedding present, so I'd bought the quilt rack in preparation for it. But that was a memory of something that would never happen.

"Maybe I should get rid of this," I said, running my hand over the white enameled rack. It had silver embellishments and was pretty enough as a piece of art. "But it's hard for me to think about that."

"Maybe you should buy a quilt you like."

"Maybe I will," I said, sticking out my tongue at the drag-onette. "What should I wear today?" Fancypants had also made himself useful as a fashion consultant. He had impec-cable taste, meaning his tastes matched mine.

"You're working today, so might I suggest the cold shoulder purple crop top and the black pleated skirt? They're pretty." He flew over and peeked in the open closet door. "Unless you want to wear a sundress. It's supposed to be near eighty today, according to what the weatherman said."

I thought about it for a moment. "I'll wear a sundress." While I loved my leather, I had a feeling I'd be seeing Faron today and he liked me in sundresses. Not to mention, if it was going to be near eighty, leather was too hot. I sorted through my clothes. I had four sundresses, and one was a vivid cobalt, which made my hair stand out.

As I hooked my bra and slid into a pair of bikini panties, Fancypants delicately turned away. We weren't the same species, but he had a sense of decorum and, unlike cats, he never followed me into the bathroom.

I finished my makeup and slid on a pair of three-inch-heeled Candies. My mother had loved them when I was younger, and I remembered playing dress-up with her wooden platformed slides. After a final glance in the mirror, I hurried to the kitchen. Grams was making oatmeal, bacon, and eggs. She motioned for me to sit down and brought me a plate with a bowl.

"Good morning, dear. You look lovely." Grams settled in at the table after serving Fancypants. She'd made him eggs and bacon, and a piece of toast. "What are you doing today? I thought I'd go into town and talk to Bree about day excur-sions around the area."

I hesitated, then said, "You suggested I join a gym to take

out some of my stress. I thought I'd drive into town before the shop opens and sign up for a membership."

"Good idea. There's nothing like working the body to relieve you of stress." Grams handed me coffee and poured her tea. "I might go out exploring this afternoon. I'll text you so you don't worry."

We finished breakfast, content in the morning warmth.

THE ONE GYM in Starwood Hollow was called Iron-Fit, and it was owned and operated by a bear shifter named Jon Elstad. He was buff, built, and bear-a-licious, dressed in a pair of compression shorts and a sweat-wicking muscle shirt. He had a buzzcut, and his muscles had muscles. Jon was also gay and had a husband who owned an accounting business. Warren was a wolf shifter, and they were both lip-smacking gorgeous. I'd met Warren through Bree, but I hadn't had the chance to meet Jon yet.

"Hey," I said from the other side of the counter. "I'm Elphyra MacPherson. I've met your husband, Warren."

Jon sized me up. "That's right. Warren mentioned a new witch moved to town. What can I do for you?"

I frowned. "I might want a gym membership." I didn't particularly, but then again, it wouldn't hurt me to get into shape and maybe Grams was right. Maybe working out would help me take out some of the anger.

Jon motioned for me to take a seat by the side of the counter. He leaned on it with his elbows. "So, what are your goals?"

I worried my lip, then said, "I want to get out some frustration and stress. I guess...lower my stress level? Increase my endurance. But I'm too wired for yoga."

He laughed. "I think a lot of us are too wired for yoga. It's a fantastic practice but it takes a certain mindset to handle it. Well, we can work up a routine to help you reduce stress, that's for sure. How often do you plan on being in the gym?"

I almost shot back "Never" but bit my tongue. "A couple times a week to start. If I try anything more extensive, I'll quit. I know myself."

Again, he laughed, but then motioned for me to join him at the counter. "Let me get some information, if you don't mind. Your name and address?"

"Elphyra MacPherson, 7863 Oak Leaf Road." I gave him my phone number and answered some basic medical questions. "I can't do anything that's going to constrict me or make me feel tied up in any way," I added. I half expected him to ask why, but he was good about typing in the information and not questioning me.

"We have three levels of membership. The first gives you access to all machines at all times of day and to the showers, but you have to rent a locker and no training or access to the pool. We'll answer questions about how to use the equipment, of course, and if we see you attempting something dangerous, we'll step in, but no personalized training. That's the Copper level. The second level—the Silver level—also gives you access to the swimming pool, and a private locker. The third level—Gold—offers you an hour a week of private training, and full use of the gym and pool. You'll also be assigned a locker."

He handed me a brochure that listed the costs for each level. There wasn't much difference in cost between the Copper and Silver levels, but the Gold Level jumped up by two hundred a month, probably to cover the private training. You could sign up for three, six, nine, or twelve months at a time.

"Eh, sign me up for Gold, for six months. That will give me time to know whether I'm really going to use everything."

I pulled out my wallet. "Month to month, or can I pay for a half year?"

"If you buy a six-month Gold membership, you have the option for paying for the entire period, or in two install-ments." Jon typed in my choice. "Your total will be $1,980.00. Or $990 if you want to pay for half today."

I grimaced. That was more than pocket change, especially if I decided to bail. "All right, here's my credit card. Let's go for the entire amount. I assume it's non-refundable?"

"Yes, and no," he said. "I offer a seven-day trial to see if you enjoy the workouts, and a chance to work with one of the trainers here. If you aren't satisfied, you can downgrade or ask for a full refund. If you change your mind after seven days, you can cancel but you won't receive a refund." He brought out a gold rubber wristband, a badge with a bar code on it, a waterproof lanyard, and a copy of the instructions. "Don't bother coming in if you're drunk—we don't allow drunk workouts. Or stoned. I don't want to carry liability insurance for idiots."

"Well, that's a good plan," I said. "Can I book a time with you in the next couple days?"

Jon glanced at his schedule as I opened my planner, and we agreed on Saturday morning at eight A.M. I dreaded it— that was too early—but then again, I didn't want to give up my evenings so I might as well try to become an early-morning gym bunny.

As I left the gym, I felt like, for good or bad, I'd started the journey into my new life.

"CAN you make me a charm to stop my husband from cheating?"

The woman on the other side of the counter was young.

She looked about twenty-four, and she had blond curly hair pulled back in a ponytail. She was wearing a yellow and brown striped dress cinched at the waist, and brown heeled pumps. She was cute as a button, and it occurred to me that any man cheating on her had to be nuts.

I glanced around the shop. One of my regulars was poring over a selection of new tarot cards. Otherwise, the shop was empty. I motioned for the girl to follow me over to the side table where I gave readings.

"Please sit down, Ms....?" I waited until she hesitantly took her place on the chair.

"Tammy. I'm Tammy Norwyle."

"Hi Tammy, I'm Elphyra. So, why don't you tell me a little bit about why you need this charm?"

She blanched, then let out a soft sigh. "Douglas and I've been married about six months, but I found lipstick on his shirt last night, and I snuck a look at his phone while he was in the shower. He's cheating on me, all right. And I know it's with his ex."

I forced myself not to grimace. "Do you know why he might be wandering?" I tried to use words and phrases that wouldn't trigger my customers unless I thought it necessary. I couldn't advise her on what to do unless I understood some of the reasons why her husband had become a philanderer.

"Several years back, before I came into the picture, they were a couple. She dumped him, and he eventually met me. I thought we were happy," she said, her eyes tearing up. "I thought that he'd left all that behind. As far as I know, she didn't contact him until he was married to me. She's engaged, and the four of us became a social foursome. But a month ago, he stayed out late and came home drunk. As I was helping him undress, I found...nail marks on his back."

"Well, one thing I can tell you is this: you can't change someone to make them love you, or to make them faithful to you. It must come from within. Is there anything missing that you think he's getting from her?"

Prying was a delicate matter, but once again—magic wouldn't work unless you knew the specifics of a situation. A prosperity spell wouldn't help long term, when you were dealing with someone who spent every dime they got.

Tammy worried her lip. "Crap," she said quietly. "He's getting something different, all right. Early on, when we were discussing our exes, he said that she was a private dominatrix at one point, and she tried out various punishments on him."

I blinked. This wasn't going to be easy. Fetishes were usually deeply ingrained and part of the personality. It wasn't an easy hill, trying to turn chocolate into vanilla. "You think he misses the kink?"

Tammy nodded, tears in her eyes. "I know he does. He looks at porn when he doesn't think I'm watching and it's all women dressed up in leather, spanking and whipping men. But I can't do that! It's not who I am. I didn't know he was really *into* it until after we were married."

I groaned. "You mean, you didn't discuss it when you talked about sex? What about when you were..." I stopped, realizing I was walking into territory she might be uncomfortable with. But if she really wanted her marriage to work, we were going to have to discuss all the aspects. "What about when the two of you were in bed?"

Tammy blushed. "I didn't...we didn't...I didn't want to sleep together until after we were married. His family was pressuring him to ask me. Apparently, I'm the closest fit to their ideal vision of a daughter-in-law, and since he's from money, he's expected to produce an heir. Now here we are, four months into the marriage, and I'm pregnant and he's cheating on me with some slut."

The words that came out of her mouth were sharp, not at all fitting with the woman sitting in front of me, but emotions could derail everything else. I had the sneaking suspicion that Douglas's love stretched to her simply because she was a good fit for the "proper mother" image he needed to appease his family.

There were only so many things I could do. Magic couldn't change someone's innate nature without breaking them. And if his preference for kink was ingrained in his nature, I wasn't going to be able to drag it out of him.

"Have you ever thought of trying to join him—not with her, but the two of you? Finding a middle ground that will work for both of you?" But I knew the answer by the look on her face.

"No," she said, staunchly shaking her head. "I can't imagine doing that. And I'm pregnant—even if I thought I could, how the hell am I going to take care of a baby and play a kink queen? He's not going to be helping me with the child. I knew that when I married him."

A little alarm rang in my head. "Why *did* you marry him? I know you didn't realize he had a fetish, but..."

"I love him," she said.

There was something else she wasn't saying. I waited.

She blushed, playing with her handbag. It was a designer clutch.

After a moment, she said, "I come from a poor family. We were rich at one time, when I was younger, but then something happened to my father's business and suddenly we weren't. But we're still considered one of the original families of Starlight Hollow."

"So you have the breeding he was looking for, but not money."

"Right. I'm twenty-four, and there was no chance for me to go to college. I tried for scholarships but they're not easy to come by and I'm not smart. I know it—I admit it. I have a sister and two brothers, all in their teens. One brother can probably get a full ride because he's good at football. But Nanda and Rick? They're smart but they can't spend their spare time volunteering or whatever else gets you a grant. All three work after-school jobs to help the family survive."

I sighed. "And your marriage will help your siblings, because your husband will fund their schooling?"

"I'm the only one who *can* help. My father ignores everything in favor of his drinking. He's one of those genteel social drinkers. My mother can't work, she's disabled."

"So you are the family's hope."

"Sometimes, you have to accept your place in life." She shrugged. "I caught the eye of somebody with money. He works for his family business and makes a good living. He's in line for a significant trust fund when he turns thirty. He'll be a good father, and I'll keep my figure and looks, and play the pretty wife on his arm at functions. He won't divorce me because his family doesn't believe in divorce. Everything will be *oh so* respectable." She hung her head, her eyes welling with tears. "But it's humiliating. He invites his mistress to dinner, and I sit there, knowing what's going on."

I had no idea what to say. How could I make things any better? "Does her fiancé know about the affair?"

She shrugged. "I don't know."

"Let me think for a few days," I said. "I'll see if I can come up with some plan." I handed her a tissue and she dabbed at her eyes. "Meanwhile, hang in there. Spend time with people who love you—your baby will need a calm mama." I walked over to one of the shelves and found a Peace of Mind candle, a spray to clear negative energy, and a beautiful rose quartz worry stone. I set them in front of her. "These will help over the next week or so as I try to figure out the best way to help."

She blew her nose. "How much do I owe you?"

"Let me ring you up," I said, stepping behind the cash

register. I had to teach myself not to keep giving away items. It was hard, but I was managing to do better—remembering that they had come to me for help in the first place, and I wasn't obliged to give them anything. "That will be $27.52."

As I ran her credit card through and she signed the receipt, I wrote down her phone number and told her I'd call whenever I figured something out.

BY CLOSING TIME AT THREE, I'd managed to book three tarot readings, schedule a consultation time with another client who wanted me to help her map out a witch's herbal garden, had sold enough sage and sage spray that I wondered if the Boogie Man had come to town, and I'd also sold the most expensive crystal ball in the shop, which tendered me a tidy sum. I armed the security system and locked the door.

As I was headed back toward the house, Faron pulled in. I groaned, thinking he'd have to meet Grams now, but as I darted up the porch steps, I saw she'd left me a note. She'd be out all afternoon, exploring the town. She'd called her hired driver to pick her up.

Clad in black jeans, with a black blazer over a blue V-neck tank top, Faron loped up the porch steps, his boots sounding with each footstep. His hair was loose, falling past his shoulders in waves, as dark as black coffee, and his eyes were as dark as his hair. He had a five o'clock shadow that made my heart race.

It was getting harder to keep my hands off him when we were together, and while he'd never pushed me, he would sweep me off to the bedroom if I gave him the signal.

He picked me up and swung me around before planting a kiss on my lips. Then he pulled away. "Hey, beautiful, glad to see me?" he asked, nuzzling my neck.

"More than glad," I said, losing myself in his arms as I felt a slick of wetness between my legs. Oh yes, I wanted him. My body ached, it had been so long since I had been held and touched and loved. I leaned into his embrace, letting him rock me gently as we stood there.

"I could get used to this," he whispered, kissing my ear.

"So could I," I whispered back. After a moment I reluctantly stood back. "Did you talk to Bree?"

"Yes, love, I did. As I thought, I couldn't pick up much, except..."

"Yes?" I asked when he paused.

"I think...there *was* a scent around the tree. Male. Like pheromones but I think it was something else." He grimaced. "I think whoever planted that camera marked the tree. It's not shifter scent, so I can't be positive."

I searched his face, not fully comprehending what he was trying to say. "You mean he peed on it?"

"Not exactly." He cleared his throat. "Whoever he was, he left a present on the trunk." When I still didn't respond, he sighed and said, "Bluntly put, the guy shot his wad there. He ejaculated on the tree. My guess is he was wanking it while watching her."

My stomach lurched. "Oh gods, I wish I hadn't asked. Did you tell her?"

He winced. "I didn't want to, but she has a right to know, especially if he ends up to be dangerous. This way, she can take extra precautions. As I said, the guy's no shifter, so we can strike the thought that he's the serial killer."

"That's not a whole lot of comfort," I said. "But I guess it's better than nothing. And there's no way to tell who the guy is?"

Faron shook his head. "Not unless you want me to walk up to every guy in the street and ask to smell his junk. And as much as I like Bree, I'm not willing to volunteer for that duty." He laughed and I joined him. It was nervous laughter on my part, but sometimes that was the easiest way to cope with things.

"No, I'm not going to ask you to do that," I said. "Why don't you come in and have some coffee?"

"Are you sure your great-grandmother won't find out who I am?" he said. He might as well have shown his teeth. I could feel the sting behind the words.

"Oh, shut up. I'm sorry. She's out right now. If she comes home, so be it. She knows I'm dating you. But she might be inclined to give you a talking-to. Don't say I didn't warn you —or try to protect you from it." I opened the screen door, waiting.

Faron followed right behind me, slapping my ass as I headed into the house. "Don't worry. I can hold my own."

I wasn't as sure as he was. In a battle of wills between the King of the Olympic Wolf Pack and my great-grandmother, my bets were on Grams, every time.

CHAPTER NINE

Faron stayed for a few minutes, but he had Pack business to get back to.

"Will you be around tonight?" he asked. "I'd like to come over."

"Not tonight. Grams and I have magical plans—she's going to help me with something that I need to do." The cord cutting ceremony was going to be hard, and I really didn't want to talk about it.

A concerned look in his eyes, Faron stroked my face. "You look worried," he said.

"I know, but—" I paused as Fancypants came careening through the living room and crashed into us. "Hey!"

"'Scuse me," he said, swooping up to fly out of the way. Three angry wasps followed him. He snorted, smoke pouring out of his nostrils. The smoke was so thick it knocked the insects for a loop, and as they dizzily spun out of the way, I grabbed the flyswatter and whacked them to the floor, where Faron stepped on them with his thick boots.

Once all three were dead, Fancypants cleared his throat.

"Thank you," he said after a moment. "I didn't mean to lead them to you."

"What *were* you doing?" Thoughts of the cord cutting vanished, replaced by the concern that I had a wasps' nest in the wall.

"I was looking for honey." Fancypants settled down on the back of the sofa. "I found a nest outside and wanted some honey."

Faron let out a strangled laugh. "Wasps don't make honey. Hornets and wasps are the assholes of the bee world. Was it a paper nest, hanging from a tree branch?"

Fancypants bobbed his head. "Yes, it was. It's on the big fir near the shed."

"I'll be right back," Faron said. "Meanwhile, teach him about honeybees." He slipped out the front door, shutting it behind him.

"Faron's right," I said turning to the dragonette. "Honey-bees live in hives. Their hives are usually inside a tree, or in the side of a house, or they live in actual hives if a beekeeper is keeping them. Faron's right—wasps are a bunch of assholes spoiling for a fight. Bees? Nice. Necessary. We'd all die without bees. Wasps? I'm not sure what they contribute to the world, but it's better to give them a wide berth."

Fancypants sighed. "I thought they all made honey."

"I have honey in the kitchen. Why did you decide to take them on? Stealing honey from wild bees isn't a nice thing to do." Fancypants was, overall, a delightful creature, but some-times his life choices confounded me.

"I don't know," he said with a shrug. Watching a drag-onette shrug was both cute and comical at the same time. "It was quicker than coming inside. Where did Faron go?"

"I'm not sure—" I stopped as Faron reentered the house.

"That's a wasps' nest, all right. I called one of my men who specializes in bees—he keeps the beehives for the commune, and he'll be down in half an hour to collect the nest. It's always best to leave these matters to the professionals." He glanced at his phone. "His name is Kyle. I have to run, I have a meeting to attend, but he'll have identification. With the serial killer still on the loose, I make all my people carry their identification."

He kissed me again, then—with a wave at Fancypants— ducked back outside. I closed the door behind him and turned to Fancypants.

"He likes you," Fancypants said.

I couldn't deny it anymore. "Yeah, he does."

"And you like him."

"Kind of." I stared at the dragonette. "Go on with you, as Grams would say. I don't want to talk about this anymore."

"You mean you don't want to make a choice. Bran likes you. Faron likes you. You like both of them."

I started to walk away but then, turned back. "I *do* like both. But just when I think I'm leaning toward Faron, Bran comes along and does something wonderful. And vice versa. They know about each other, it's not like I'm lying to them, or hiding anything from them."

"Then, until—*unless*—you decide to commit to *one* of them, you don't have to worry, right?"

I wanted to agree, but the fact was, I didn't know if I could sustain two relationships. And I was afraid of losing their friendship. I didn't know how Bran or Faron would react once I took the relationship with the other to a physical level.

A knock on the door interrupted me and I breathed a sigh of relief, pushing my thoughts away. I opened the door to find a tall, sturdy man standing there, wearing a cowboy hat. He held out a Pack identification badge and his license, showing him to be Kyle Collinsworth.

"Kyle? The bee man? Are you Faron's brother?" I could see a resemblance between the two in their facial structure.

"Yeah, actually I am. Faron said you have a problem with wasps?"

I pointed toward the tree in question. "There. A wasps' nest is apparently hanging on a branch. I didn't notice it this morning, but...yeah, wasps. Would you like coffee or something?"

He shook his head. "No thank you, ma'am. I'll take care of the wasps. Do you want the nest for some sort of spell work?"

I thought about it for a moment. "Maybe a few parts of it. But none of the wasps. They're such creepy little critters."

He gave me a polite smile. "I'll take care of it. You should probably stay inside till I'm done. It will take about twenty minutes." He tipped his hat and headed for the fir tree. I watched for a moment before closing the door.

I immediately texted Grams with instructions not to come into the yard during the next half hour, lest the wasps—indignant that they were losing their home—swarm her. She texted back that she would be home in an hour and was making dinner.

Stuck inside, I called Bree. "Hey, how are you? Faron told me what he found out."

She made a disgusted sound. "I wanted to vomit. How gross was that? And if he's been watching me for a while, does he have video? What about when I..." She fell silent for a moment.

"Masturbate? It's okay, we all do it."

"Yeah, we do, but not for an *audience*!" She sounded mortified. "What if he uploaded those pictures somewhere? What if I'm out there on the net, naked? Or worse?"

I wanted to calm her down. She was starting to spiral, and it wasn't like Bree to spiral. "Hey, catch your breath. If he's so obsessed, chances are he'll want to keep those pictures all for himself. He won't want to share them!"

She hiccupped. "You think so?"

"I *know* so," I said. I didn't, but that didn't matter right now. Bree needed something to hold onto, and that was the best thing I could think of. "Did you talk to Daisy again?"

"Yeah. She sent out an officer to take prints around where we found the cameras. They also had me look through a book of mug shots of sex offenders. *That* was a delight. At least it wasn't a bunch of selfies. But I didn't recognize any of them —" she paused. "Hold on, someone's at the door. I'll call you right back."

I curled up on the sofa, waiting. Five minutes later, the phone rang.

"Hey, who was it?"

"I don't know," Bree said, her voice shaking. "There was nobody there, but there was a box on my porch. Elphyra, it's a bouquet of dead roses. They're falling apart."

I tensed. "Is there a card?"

"Yeah. I'm afraid to open it."

"Then wait. I'm coming over." I jumped up and, with Fancypants flying behind me, I grabbed my keys and purse and cautiously exited the house. It looked like Kyle was keeping the action by the tree. I waved to him and motioned to myself and the car. He waved back as I fastened my seatbelt. Fancypants settled himself on the passenger seat and I helped him into the dragonette-sized harness I'd rigged up for him. Before pulling out of the driveway, I texted Grams.

I'M HEADED OVER TO BREE'S HOUSE. SHE'S IN A STATE— SOMETHING'S GOING ON. I'LL TRY TO BE HOME BEFORE YOU GET THERE BUT IF I'M NOT, I'LL TEXT YOU MORE.

GO WITH NO WORRIES. DINNER WILL TAKE ME AN HOUR TO MAKE. FEEL FREE TO INVITE HER TO EAT. SHE CAN STAY

FOR THE CORD CUTTING IF YOU'D LIKE—IF SHE'S UP FOR IT.
IN FACT, IT MIGHT HELP TO HAVE A GOOD FRIEND THERE.

THANKS. HEADING OUT NOW. KYLE'S ALMOST DONE WITH
THE WASPS.

BREE WAS WAITING at the door. As she unlocked it and let
me in, Oscar and Atlas crowded close to her. Their ears on
alert, they looked ready to pounce. It was obvious they sensed
something was up.

I gave her a tight hug. "Show me the flowers."

She led me over to the coffee table, where a long square
box rested. It was open. The ribbon that had tied it shut was
black, and inside was a full bouquet of dead burgundy roses. A
card sat on the table next to it. I didn't touch the box or the
card. I didn't want to disrupt any fingerprints. The card read:

You spoiled my surprise, you, who fill my eyes,
    Every waking moment, within my heart you lie.
    I would be your King, I would be your savior,
    I would be your everything, you, my sacred treasure.
    Don't push me away, I won't let you go,
    The harder you resist, the darker I'll grow.
    I am the moth to your luminous sun,
    We're wedded in soul, we're already one.
    I'm waiting for you. Don't disappoint me again.
Don't try to get away. I'll always be watching you. If I
see that wolf shifter at your house again, I'll dismember
him piece by piece and then I'll have to punish you.
And I don't want to have to punish you.

I looked over at her. Bree's face was white.

"He must have seen Faron arrive. How? We took down the cameras! And why didn't I know that I was being watched? I have excellent hunting skills. I can track and find my way through the wilderness. How did I miss this?" She shook her hands. "I can't shake the feeling that, although we found the bugs the other day, he can still hear and see me." As she gasped, hyperventilating, I took her by the shoulders and walked her over to the sofa.

"Sit. Breathe." I closed my eyes and smoothed the energy in her aura. It was flaring, like the sun, and the more it flared, the more frantic she became. I coaxed up my own energy— the healing, soothing energy of the earth—a furl of green smoke with gold sparkles running through it.

"What am I going to do?"

"Close your eyes and let me work."

Bree sat back, trying to relax. Her energy wasn't as strong as mine was, given mine was infused with magic, and so I sent the earth element through her aura, soothing the fear. The swirling earth energy smoothed out the wisps of fear and she started to breathe easier.

After a few minutes, she managed to gain control of her emotions, and she let out a long sigh and shook her head. "Okay, Daisy needs to see what he sent me. I'll call her."

"I need to tell Faron to be careful. If this freak decides to go off on him..."

"Please do. And apologize for me."

"Apologize? You don't have anything to be sorry about. You're not the one at fault." I paused, not wanting to leave her alone. "Say, do you want to come over for dinner? Grams is helping me tonight with a cord cutting ceremony to let go of Rian."

Bree thought about it for a moment. "I don't want to be in the way."

"You won't be. Call Daisy and see when she can be here."

Bree pulled out her cell phone and called the sheriff. While she did that, I texted Faron, telling him what was going on, then texted Grams, telling her Bree would be joining us. Grams texted back immediately, saying there would be plenty of dinner.

A moment later, Bree hung up. "Daisy's in the neighborhood. She'll be here in five minutes." She stared at the dead flowers and the note. "You want to hear something?"

"What is it?"

"For the first time in my life, I think I'm scared."

AFTER DAISY ARRIVED and took the evidence into custody, telling Bree she might want to get a security system, Bree followed me over to my house. I told her to bring the dogs. She would worry about them being home alone, especially with a crazed stalker on the loose.

We drove back to my place, Bree following me, and the first thing I noticed was that Kyle had left a note stating the wasps were gone. There might be a few flying around, he warned me, but he had managed to take the nest. He promised to give Faron some of the paper from it once he had evicted all the tenants.

Grams's hired car pulled in as I was unlocking the door. As she stepped out, I motioned for Fancypants to go inside, and Bree and I hurried to take the grocery bags from her. Grams also had a couple other shopping bags and refused to let me carry them.

"I'm perfectly capable of carrying these. Now, get those bags into the kitchen so I can start making dinner," she said, shooing us into the house. As I carried the food into the kitchen, I heard Grams say to Bree, "You look as shaken as a martini. What's wrong?"

Bree spoke in soft tones that I couldn't quite make out as I unloaded the food. There was fresh-caught wild salmon, potatoes, heavy cream, extra-sharp cheddar, chives and shallots, fresh peas, a box of imported shortbread mix, and strawberries.

I had finished setting the food on the counter when Grams entered the kitchen, a look of concern filling her eyes.

"Bree told me what happened. It's dangerous for her to stay there alone."

"I know," I said. At that moment, my phone sounded. It was Faron, texting me back.

WHAT THE FUCK? IF HE SETS A FOOT NEAR ME, HE'LL FIND OUT WHY PEOPLE FEAR WOLF SHIFTERS. YOU ASK BREE IF SHE WANTS ME TO POST A COUPLE GUARDS ON HER LAND. NOBODY BUT NOBODY IS GOING TO INTIMIDATE ME, AND ANY FREAK WHO TREATS A WOMAN THIS WAY NEEDS TO BE HORSEWHIPPED. MY CREW AND I ARE READY TO HELP.

LET ME ASK HER. WE SHOULD PROBABLY ASK DAISY, AS WELL.

TEXT ME ONCE YOU DO.

I slid off my stool. "I'll be right back. I need to talk to Bree. After that, I'll help you cook."

"No, don't worry about cooking. I want to make dinner."

I kissed her on the cheek. "Thanks." I knew Grams was an excellent cook. My mother valued good cooking and that was one of the few good things she had to say about my great-grandma. "I'm going to check on Bree."

"Off with you, girl." Grams tied an apron around her waist —she'd brought her own—and deftly opened packages and chose pots and pans.

Bree was curled on my sofa, the dogs at her feet. Fancypants was awkwardly patting her shoulder. I sat down next to her.

"Faron has offered to have a couple of his men patrol your yard. Would you like that?"

She shifted, crossing her legs in the lotus pose. "That's nice of him. I *would* feel safer if there was somebody there with me. What do you think Daisy would say?"

"Call her and ask. If she can't post someone at your house 24/7, then maybe it's wise to bring in Faron's men. I warned him to be careful." I reached down to scratch Oscar behind the ears. He let out a *hrmph* and looked up at me, expectant. "I'm sorry, I don't have any treats."

Bree pulled out her phone and called Daisy. "Hey, this is Bree Loomis... Yeah, I am... Listen, Faron offered to keep several of his men on my land to watch out for me. What do you think?" She waited a moment, then said, "Right. Okay, thank you... Yeah, it will make me feel better."

As she ended the call, Bree looked down at the dogs. "Hey guys, what do you think about having a couple wolves help us out?" She glanced at me. "The sheriff thinks it's a good idea. She doesn't have the manpower to keep someone at my house, and she doesn't think I should be alone right now."

"Then I'll text Faron," I said. He quickly replied that he'd be over in a few minutes, and I invited him to dinner.

"I'm going to help Grams. I don't think I can sit still," she said. She jumped up and headed into the kitchen before I could stop her.

TWENTY MINUTES LATER, the doorbell rang. When I told Grams that Faron was joining us, she merely looked at me for a moment, then said, "Well, set another plate. There's plenty of food." I couldn't tell if she was irritated or being her usual brusque self.

Faron had spiffed himself up. He was wearing a black suede sports jacket over a pale blue button-down shirt, along with black jeans and his usual motorcycle boots. His hair was pulled back in a long ponytail, and he had shaved. I slowly moved toward him, unable to look away. The man was like a beacon to me. He opened his arms and I stepped into his embrace, breathing in his spicy aroma as I leaned against him.

"I feel safe in your arms," I whispered.

"I will always protect you," Faron said, kissing my forehead. "But for the moment, I don't want your great-grandmother to see me pawing you."

"You're not pawing," I said.

"I want to." He slid his hand down my back to cup my ass, then quietly let go. "Come on, introduce me to your great-grandmother. What should I call her?"

"Why don't you start with 'Ms. MacPherson'?" I said, taking him by the hand and leading him toward the kitchen. I took a deep breath, and—hoping Grams would behave—led him into the lion's den.

CHAPTER TEN

Dinner went as well as I could hope, given the circumstances. The food was delicious—grilled salmon, scalloped potatoes in a shallot and chive cream sauce, fresh peas, and strawberry shortcake with cheese wedges. The food was so good that we barely spoke during the meal, except for Fancypants, who happily slurped his way through three servings. The only sounds other than the dragonette were the clinking sounds of silverware against china.

Faron glanced at Fancypants and laughed. "You're going to grow up and weigh as much as a Komodo the way you're tucking it in."

"I do like my food," Fancypants said, wiping his chin as cream sauce dribbled down to splatter on the plate.

"Yes, you do. And so do I. Ms. MacPherson, this is delicious. I've never had salmon cooked this way. I'd love to give the recipe to my housekeeper." He ended it on a question, rather than as a statement.

She studied him for a moment, then let out a sigh. "All right. I'll write out the recipe for you to take home. Shall we have our dessert in the living room?"

I had no problem allowing Grams to take over the lead. Actually, I was starting to enjoy having her stay with me. I felt protected with her around. While I loved my privacy, Grams had brought a sense of safety to my life. And Faron, he was beginning to feel safe to me as well.

As we relaxed with our dessert, Grams questioned Faron. She was polite, albeit distant. He answered her politely, treating her with respect. We tiptoed around topics including the town, the area, Faron's community. Grams was courteous to Faron. He reciprocated. Finally, Grams set her dessert plate on the coffee table.

"Well, Faron, my great-granddaughter seems to have developed a fondness for you."

"Grams!" I sat straight, blushing.

"It's true, you can't deny it. And I *will* have my say. Your mother isn't here to do so, and even if she was, she wouldn't have the strength." She turned to Faron. "It's hard for me to approve, given the differences in our lineages. But you seem respectful, congenial, and you *are* a king. That will be a plus, should the two of you get serious."

"Grams, we're just dating—" I started to say.

Faron was looking like she had tightened a noose around his neck. In a strained voice, he said, "Thank you." It came out as a question, but I couldn't blame him for that.

Bree intervened. "Faron, I'm going to take you up on your offer. I don't know if Elphyra told you or not—"

"She did, which is why I'm here. If you don't mind," he added, turning to me, "I'd like to have two of my officers come over to meet Bree. We can brief them without the fear of being watched, and they can escort her home."

"I want to go with you and spend the night," I said to Bree. Although she was going to have security, she was still upset, and I wanted to be there for her.

"Then I'll go as well. I'll stand guard with my officers.

They can keep watch for at least a week—if not more. We'll figure it out. We're not going to leave you alone," Faron added.

I glanced over at Grams, surprised to see her nod appreciatively.

While Faron called the commune, I ducked into my bedroom to pack an overnight bag. Bree hadn't bothered to protest, which told me how upset this whole mess had made her.

Grams insisted on packing up extra desserts for Faron's security force, as well as for the three of us. "You'll want a little extra for before bedtime. Bree, why don't you go ask Fancypants if he's staying here or going with you, so I can tuck in a bite for him as well."

Bree vanished back into the living room.

Grams turned to me. "Are you sure it's wise to get yourself mixed up in this? I understand she's your best friend, but if you get this pervert angry at you, he might aim his sights on *you*, as well."

I worried my lip. "I know that's a possibility. But Bree's my buddy, Grams. She's my heart. She has my back and I have hers."

"Then I want you to take this," she said, reaching in the folds of her pocket. She brought out what looked like a pocketknife, but she held it to the side and pressed a button. A narrow, wicked-looking blade popped out.

"You have a *switchblade*? That's illegal!"

"The cops won't know if you don't tell them," she said, winking at me. "Take this and keep it on you, within easy reach. It's easier to pay a fine than to want for a good blade."

I stared at her, not sure what to think or say. Grams was a woman who could take care of herself—she carried that sturdy, Highlands blood in her veins. *Strict, stern, and sturdy,* my mother called it. But I had thought my great-grand-mother was more conscientious about rules and laws.

"What?" she asked as I continued to stare. "You think I made it to over a hundred years old without a little help in my purse?"

Again, I didn't answer. But as I pocketed the knife, the doorbell rang. I went to answer it, but Faron had gotten there before me, and he ushered in a man and a woman, both muscled and somber.

"Meet Claudette and Lief. They're sergeants in my Pack. They'll be guarding your land and house during the night," he said to Bree. "We'll switch out come morning."

Bree licked her lips. "I'm pleased to meet you. Thank you. I really hate imposing—"

"Don't worry, ma'am. Lord Faron has assured us this is a life-or-death situation. We won't let anybody in. If you don't mind me suggesting," Claudette said, "when we get to your house, please allow us to secure the yard and the house before you get out of the car."

She sounded all business, and by her stance, I could tell she was used to being respected.

Bree let out a long breath, relaxing. "Thank you. I'm so frazzled—"

"Ma'am, we'll be on the job. You can sleep easy tonight. Now, if you would introduce us to your dogs so that they understand we're friends," Lief said. He was kind of cute, I thought, with chin-length curly red hair and bright blue eyes.

"Of course," Bree said. She stepped forward and called Oscar and Atlas over, introducing them to the pair. She also introduced the dogs to Faron. "Boys, these people are going to protect us, so please treat them nicely."

Oscar woofed. Atlas wagged his tail.

"Do you want me to translate?" Fancypants asked, landing on the floor next to the dogs.

I blinked. In fact, everybody did a doubletake. "Is that a *thing*? You can speak to dogs?"

"And cats, and cows...dolphins. Owls. A few other species. Not in the way *we* talk, but yes, I can communicate." He preened a little and I tried not to laugh.

"I should have called you 'Dr. Dolittle,' " I said.

He gave me a blank look. "Doctor who?"

"No, not Dr. Who—Dr. Dolittle."

"Who's Dolittle?"

I started to answer, but decided to just take pity on the little guy. He looked confused enough as it was. "Don't worry about it. I'll tell you later. It refers to a movie. But if you can communicate with animals, then would you tell the dogs that Claudette and Lief are friends, and they're going to help protect Bree?"

"I can do that." Fancypants flew down to the floor and waddled—when they were on the ground, dragonettes often waddled like penguins—over to Oscar. He let out a couple guttural sounds that sounded like a cross between a bark and a grunt. A moment later, Atlas whined and walked over to Claudette, where he licked her hand. Oscar followed.

"Done. Concepts like that are easier to translate, though. Don't ask me to ask them what they think about a movie." Fancypants took to the air—he bent his knees and gave a little jump, his wings kicking in the moment he left the floor —and flew back to join me.

"Thank you," Bree said. "I feel like I'm causing everybody a lot of trouble."

Bree was usually so pulled together and independent that it hurt me to see her so vulnerable. I headed back into the kitchen, where Grams had finished stacking the dishwasher and was putting the food away.

"About the cord cutting ceremony—"

"Obviously, tonight would be best. It's the new moon," she said. "But we can make do."

"Will it really matter what phase of the moon we're in?" I asked.

"Well, this isn't something I'd do after the waxing half-crescent," she said. "But we have a few days we can work within until then. You go. I'll stay here with Fancypants." She wiped her hands on a towel and untied her apron.

"Do you want to come with us? I'm sure Bree wouldn't mind."

"No, child. I'm going to perform a new moon ritual, since the house will be empty. I'll be raiding your herb garden, if you don't mind." She kissed my cheek. "Be careful. But I'll rest easier knowing your young man and his entourage are watching over you."

I laughed. "He's not such a 'young man.' Faron's a shifter. He's likely nearing your age."

"Shifters age slowly. He's still young in all the ways that count. Anyway, go and tend to your friend." She waved me off, making certain I had the basket filled with the extra strawberry shortcakes. After saying good night to Fancypants, we trouped out, and—in a caravan of cars—headed toward Bree's house.

I WOKE up several times that night, peeking out the window. I couldn't see the shifters out there, but I could sense Faron. We'd grown close enough that he was on my magical radar. The dogs were in Bree's bedroom, where they should be, and they were quiet all night.

Morning came early, and I was up by seven-thirty. But Bree was already in the kitchen making breakfast. Stacks of pancakes covered the table, along with a huge platter of scrambled eggs and a tray of sausage links.

"Can you call them in?" she asked.

I peeked out the door and whistled. Within minutes, Faron, Claudette, and Lief crowded into the kitchen. They reported no issues as we all sat down to breakfast.

"The relief crew will be here in ten minutes," Faron said. "I also have recruited a volunteer to stay with you at your workplace. She'll meet you there—her name is Veronique. The men coming this morning are Paris and Lief's brother, Hans."

Claudette spoke up. "Lief and I'll be back tonight around eight to relieve Hans and Paris. We didn't see anything, though I doubt we will, if your stalker realizes you're being protected."

"At some time, I guess we'll have to draw him out—" Bree started to say.

"Yes, but first, we want to make certain you're secure," Faron said. "All right, let's finish breakfast and then get home for a little shut-eye. I won't be back tonight, I have too many things to attend to, but Claudette and Lief are perfectly capable of handling this case."

"I need to stay home tonight, too. But call if you need me," I added.

"I'll be all right," she said, straightening her shoulders. "Last night I was really freaked, but I'm better this morning. Thank Fancypants for me again for talking to the dogs."

"I will." I gave her a hug and headed out toward my car. Faron followed me. Claudette and Lief stayed so they could introduce Hans and Paris to Bree.

Faron wrapped his arms around my waist. "You know, in the middle of everything that was happening last night, do you remember that your grandmother gave us her tacit approval?"

"Yeah, I do."

I didn't know why I was feeling hesitant—I had wanted her approval. When she met Bran, she'd obviously been hopeful that he and I would grow more serious. I liked Bran —he was extremely attractive. He was sweet and helpful. But right now, I had to admit, Faron had the edge. There was something about him that stirred up the butterflies in my stomach.

"I'll see you later," I said, leaning up to kiss him. He wrapped one arm around my waist. As his tongue played in my mouth, I softly moaned, my resistance and will slipping. Every inch of me wanted him.

I finally managed to break away, though gently, and touched him on the nose. "I'll see you later," I whispered. Then, before he could answer, I jumped into my car.

I WAS on the way home to get ready for work when I saw the sheriff's car parked by the side of the road. Daisy was standing next to it, and when she looked up and saw my car, she raised one hand to flag me down. She was parked in a turnout, which led to a walking trail through a woody thicket called Taylor's Gulch. It wasn't really a gulch, though it *was* a ravine—one of those common here in the wilds of western Washington, with steep sides overgrown with ferns and brambles and stinging nettle that led down to a lazy creek.

Thimble Creek meandered through the thicket, which covered a four-hundred-acre patch. Well-trod trails and paths offered plenty of exercise for hikers and horses alike. The elevation rose abruptly, for Taylor's Gulch was an oxymoron and was located on a hill. While most of the walking trails were easy enough, there were a handful that only the most determined attempted. Those led through tougher terrain, and the paths were rough and precarious.

I slowed down and jumped out of the car, heading over to her side. "Hey, I just came from Bree's. Faron has stationed two members of his company to watch over her land and she'll have someone at the shop with her."

"That's good. I think we may have a break in the case, but right now, it has to go on the backburner." She was so pale I thought she might faint.

I glanced toward the woods. Crime tape cordoned off the entrance to the thicket, and another officer was marking off the entrance to the parking lot. There were three other patrol cars there, along with the coroner's car. *Crap.* "Another murder?"

"Yes. If we don't find him soon, the vigilantes are going to be out in force and then we're going to be in real trouble. This is our sixth victim, with the fourth never identified. I imagine this is how the cops felt with the Green River Killer —he went on and on and on." Daisy rubbed her forehead.

"Who is it this time? Or is that private information?"

"It's private for now. But I was wondering..." She drifted off, looking uncomfortable.

"Do you want me to see if the ghost is around?" I asked. "If I can talk to the victim's spirit?"

"That would help, yes. But I need to prepare you—this one's different." There were tears in her eyes. I was alarmed. Daisy was a tough woman, a puma shifter, like Bree, and puma shifters were resilient.

"What's wrong? What's happened? Did you know the victim?" All I could think is that whoever died must have been a friend of hers.

But she shook her head. "No, not personally," she said, her voice choked up. "But it's a child, Elphyra. *A little girl.* I want to strangle her parents for letting her out alone. They can't have missed all the warnings. They can't be that stupid."

"Blame on the murderer, Daisy. Take a deep breath. Maybe she slipped out—kids do that. Parents should know where their kids are, but sometimes that doesn't happen." I put my hand on her arm, willing the same earth energy that I'd used to calm Bree to flow through Daisy.

She blinked, looking startled, then caught her breath. "What are you doing?"

"Giving you a space in which to breathe." I glanced toward the woods again. "I don't want to go in there, but I will. And I hope, for all our sakes, that her spirit's still there."

Daisy hesitated for a moment, then motioned for one of her officers to join us. I was pleasantly surprised to see that it was Arnie Fryer. He had driven me around to some of the murder scenes before, and he was a sensitive deputy who loved his family. He also had the knack of putting people at ease.

"Hey, Arnie," I said.

"Elphyra—good to see you again, although I'm sorry it's under these circumstances," he said. I shook his hand, smiling.

Daisy turned to him. "I'd like you to escort Elphyra to the crime scene. She's going to scope out the area to see if the spirit of the girl is still around. Make certain you don't disturb any evidence. Give her all the time she needs."

"Of course," he said, turning to me. "Come with me, please."

He led me toward the trailhead. As we approached the entry into Taylor's Gulch, I tried to steel myself. Children's deaths were especially difficult, though speaking to their spirits wasn't usually as hard as seeing their remains. Knowing they survived whatever killed them offered a form of consolation, which was why some psychics made their living as liaisons between the living and the dead.

At the edge of the parking lot, the asphalt ended at the beginning of a path wide enough for two people to comfortably stroll side by side. A trail sign, rust-proof metal painted green with an acrylic enclosed sign board, had a map displaying the system of trails through Taylor's Gulch. We were about to set foot on Cedar Rain Path.

The scent of cedar hung heavy in the air, warm and musky, and I could imagine how it smelled during the rain. Petrichor was a special scent that coiled in the air in this area of Western Washington for months on end during the rainy season—that pungent tang of soil mingling with the crisp scent of tree needles with overtones of decay from the mushrooms and moss that filled the forest biome.

As Arnie escorted me onto the trail, a heavy sense of gloom descended around me. Although the sun was out, it didn't penetrate the canopy of trees very well and the path was cloaked in shadows. My pulse raced as we headed along the gently inclining path. It wasn't enough to really notice unless you raced along at a good pace. I had been walking along the trail before, early when I moved to Starlight Hollow, but it had been a while since I'd been here.

The silence deepened as we forged deeper into the gulch. The ravine wasn't visible from here; it was farther into the thicket. We paused at a fork in the trail.

"Where does this go?" I asked, indicating to the turnoff we were about to take.

Arnie took off his hat and wiped his forehead. "It's a dead-end, leading into a culvert. That's where we found her."

"How did you find her?" I asked, not wanting to hear the story, but it might help me when I came to the murder scene.

"Last night, we received a missing person's report. Sarah Smith vanished on her way home from the swimming pool at the Community Center. She was eight years old, and she had gone with friends. But when she wasn't home by dinner, her mother—Casey—called the other mothers."

Arnie sighed and continued. "When the parents of Sarah's friends asked their children if Sarah was with them, they admitted that she had insisted on stopping to buy some comic books. She told them she'd catch up, but she never did. None of the kids wanted to get her in trouble with her parents, so they didn't say anything."

"Which means there was plenty of time for someone to abduct her before she was noticed missing," I said.

"Right. She left for the pool around two o'clock and was supposed to be home by six. The kids left the pool at five-fifteen. Her parents called us at seven. So, there had been an hour and a half in which for her to vanish. Tommy's Comics & Games closes at six, and the proprietor said she left around five forty-five. He was the last to see her alive, that we know of." Arnie pointed out a rock. "Be cautious. You don't want to turn an ankle."

"How did you know to look for her here?"

"A jogger out for an early run found her this morning. It's the serial killer again." He squinted. "I can't... When it's a child, I want to quit and move to a tropical island where I never have to face another murder case again. I want to quit and go play Santa Claus year-round. And on my dark days, I want to go all Batman-vigilante and take out the bad guys without repercussions."

I didn't try to tell him he was making a difference. I understood what that dark place was like, and sometimes, you had no choice except to acknowledge the feelings and work through them.

"Are we close?"

He pointed up ahead. "Around the other side of that big cedar. Are you ready?"

I took a deep breath. "No, I'm never ready for this. But that doesn't matter, does it? You need my help. I'm here. I'll do what I can."

As he held the branches back, I plunged through, fully opening my senses. As I passed the massive cedar, I sensed a spirit near me. I glanced around at the scene. It appeared to be chaos, with the coroner's team bagging pieces of... I turned away before I could gag. Luckily, I had missed seeing the worst of the savagery, but there was blood everywhere, and I caught sight of a little purse—a popular pony character.

The purse hit me in the gut. That, right there, told me everything I needed to know about Sarah. There was a certain type of little girl who loved Precious PonyTail, and she should never, ever, meet the big bad wolf in the woods.

I saw her, over by a huckleberry bush, staring wide-eyed at the workers. She looked my way, and I raised my hand in a little wave. The girl—dressed in a one-piece swimsuit—looked confused, but she ran over to me.

Can you help me? I've been trying to find my way home but I don't know the way.

She sounded so hopeful that my heart dropped. How could I explain to her that she was dead? That she'd never sit in her mother's lap again, she'd never have dinner with her family again, that she wouldn't grow up to live her life as it extended out in front of her. At least not in this lifetime.

CHAPTER ELEVEN

I TRIED TO SUPPRESS MY TEARS. "I NEED TO TALK TO YOU.
You're Sarah, right?"

She nodded. *Mommy tells me never to talk to strangers, but you
seem nice.*

"I'm safe. It's okay to talk to me. Sarah, do you remember
going into the comic book shop?"

She scrunched up her face. *Yeah, I think I do. It seems like a
long time ago, though.*

Time worked differently on the spirit realm. After passing
through the Veil, time vanished, but in that interim space—
that liminal realm in which the dead still walked the earth—
time phased in and out. Often, spirits couldn't tell *when*
something happened, only that it *had* happened.

"And where did you go after the comic book shop?" I
motioned to Arnie. "Can you take notes? I'm talking to her
spirit now."

Arnie pulled out a notebook. "You're sure it's Sarah?"

"Yes. She remembers going to the comic shop. But she
doesn't know she's..." I paused. If I said "dead" there was a

113

chance she'd hear me. Spirits didn't always hear what the living were saying. Some heard what was asked directly of them, while others could hear what was going on around them. But I wasn't sure about Sarah, and I didn't want her startled until I broke the news to her.

Arnie glanced at me and mouthed the word "dead" and I gave him a nod.

"Right. Watch what you say, please." I turned back to Sarah. "So, do you remember anybody who stopped to talk to you after you left the comic shop?"

Sarah looked at her hands, then to the side. *Why is it so misty? Where am I?*

I tried to prompt her again. "Honey, can you focus? I'll explain everything in a moment, but I need to know if you remember the time after you left the comic shop."

She met my gaze, and the confusion shifted to fear. *I was late. I knew Mom was going to be mad, so I took a shortcut through one of the empty lots.*

"Do you remember which street that lot was on?"

After a pause, she said, *Yew Street—the corner where it meets Hemlock. There's an empty lot. My mother told me not to cut through the lot because it's so overgrown. But it's so much quicker and I thought it wouldn't hurt, not just this once.*

I turned to Arnie. "She took a shortcut through the empty lot at Yew and Hemlock." As I turned back to Sarah, her expression was quickly changing. She was looking alarmed now.

I was partway through when... A panicked look crossed her face. *He came out from behind one of the trees so fast. I didn't know what was happening. He grabbed me and I screamed, but then he put something over my nose and I couldn't breathe. Then I guess I fell asleep.*

I relayed to Arnie that the killer might have chloroformed

her. To Sarah, I asked, "Do you remember what the man looked like?"

Her eyes wide, she said, *He was short—around your height. He was thin but he was strong, and he had short gray hair and light brown eyes. He felt odd. My mom told me if somebody feels scary, even if they haven't done anything, trust my gut and run away. But I couldn't run. After I fell asleep, I woke up in the parking lot, in a van, and my hands were tied.*

She froze, and I stepped closer. I could tell she was starting to panic. "You say he had a van? What can you tell me about it?"

Yeah, he had a van. He parked near the trail. I saw it when I woke up as he was taking me out of it. It was pale blue. I remember because it was so shimmery. I saw part of the license plate. I remember numbers really well.

I straightened. If we could get a partial plate, it was far more than we'd had before. "Please tell me."

There were three letters and then the word "pig"...I think the first three letters had a "k" in the middle.

I quickly told Arnie, "I have a partial plate for you."

He wrote down the letters. "If this pans out, it could break open the case."

"Anything else, sweetie?" I asked. "Did he say anything?"

When I woke up, I was... I was on the ground, and he was standing over me. Only he looked different—he was changing into something else. Into a monster. I was so scared and I tried to cry but he had taped my mouth shut. He said, "Old Joe's going to take care of you, real good." I tried to get up, but I couldn't. He tied my feet up. She sniffled, tears tracing down her cheeks. *I remember—he turned into a monster—and he had horrible claws, and his teeth were so big and he looked like a scary man with long fur and long arms...*

"Honey, listen to me. You're okay now. You're fine now. Stop trying to remember—"

He used his claws and he swung at me and my stomach hurt so bad, and then he was growling and then…everything blurred and I felt a sharp pain in my chest. I was floating, and after that… I want to go home. I want my mommy! She threw her arms forward, trying to hug me, and went through me, landing on the ground. As she raised her head, she suddenly cried out. *I died, didn't I? He killed me? I'll never see my family again!*

I was crying now, and I knelt beside her. "Listen to me. I can tell your mommy and your family anything you want me to tell them. I know they love you and they want you to be happy. I can talk to them for you." My heart ached. I wanted to hug her, to hold her so she would feel safe. Then I thought of something. "You know something? You're a heroine. You've given me information so that we can catch him and stop him from doing this to anybody else."

She looked so forlorn that I wondered if I'd be able to help her over the Veil.

I am?

She had been such a cute little girl, and what the killer had done to her hit me in the gut. "You helped us so much, Sarah."

My mommy will be so mad that I disobeyed her.

"No, she won't be mad at you," I said, shaking my head. "She loves you more than you can imagine. She's going to miss you, but she'll be so proud of what you told me. I know this. Do you believe me?" I wiped my eyes and, using my magic, I stroked the outline of her aura, calming the fear and the sadness.

She took a deep breath. *I love her too. I love Daddy. Will you tell them that? And what's going to happen to my kitty, Sirius? I miss him already!*

"Don't you worry—I'll make certain Sirius is happy and taken care of, no matter what. And I'll let your mommy know you're okay—" I paused as another figure approached. Another spirit. I stood as the older lady walked toward us.

But Sarah turned and she gasped and raced over to the ghost.

Grandma! I thought...you're here! Did you come to help me?

I stood ready to intervene, not sure if the spirit was malign and trying to disguise herself as someone safe, but then I looked into *Grandma's* eyes and they were clear and genuine. There was no deception here. This was Sarah's grandmother.

Sarah grabbed her grandmother by the hand and dragged her over to me. *Grandma, this lady has been helping me. She says I'm a heroine!*

Grandma gazed at me for a moment. *Thank you,* she said. *My little Sarah, I'm here to take you to meet your grandpa and your older sister, Lila. And we have a kitty named Tank.* To me, she said, *I watch over the family and when Sarah...passed...I felt her pain and came looking for her. She couldn't see me till you started to talk to her.*

I let out a long breath, relieved. "What's your name?"

Adele. And in case she wants proof, will you tell my daughter that I always knew she took the ruby ring—and that it's okay. And tell her I'm watching over Sarah now, too. That I'll take care of her. She glanced over her shoulder. *We have to go now. Did Sarah tell you everything she needed to?*

I licked my lips. "Sarah, you mentioned the man said the name Joe...did he say any other name?"

Sarah thought for a moment. Then she shook her head. *No, but I saw a letter in the back of his van when I woke up. I think the name on the envelope was Joe Gregor. I remember the last name because a boy at school has the same last name. That's all.*

I smiled at her. "Okay, Sarah. I'm so glad your grandma is here. I'll talk to your parents. And always remember—they love you very much."

As Adele led Sarah away, the little girl began to chatter about all the things that had happened since Adele had died.

A moment later, they faded out of sight, vanishing like a puff of smoke.

DAISY WAS over the moon when I gave her all the information.

"This could solve the case. We'll have to go about this carefully so we follow all the rules, since we can't use this information in court. But we'll figure out a way to find him!" There was hope in her eyes for the first time in a while.

"I'm grateful Sarah's grandmother showed up. I'd like to talk to the parents, if I could."

"If you could come down to the station, I'll call them. I have to break the news, and maybe you can help them manage this. I hope I never have to inform another family that this fucker has killed one of their children." Daisy headed toward her car. "The coroner and my men can finish up here."

I agreed to follow her to the station.

WHILE I WAS at the station, I called Grams. "Can you open the shop today? The spare key is in the righthand drawer next to the sink, in the kitchen. I'll fill you in when I get home. It's too complicated to explain now."

"Are you all right? Is Bree all right?"

"We're both fine, yes. This has nothing to do with Bree's situation."

"All right. Do you have any specials going on that I should know about?"

I thought for a moment. "No, not that I can think of. Thanks, Grams. You're a lifesaver."

Talking to Sarah's parents was harder than I imagined. The realization that their little girl had been murdered by a serial killer was worse than the knowledge that Sarah was dead. The air was thick with anger and self-recriminations when I went to talk to them after Daisy had informed them of their daughter's death.

Daisy had asked me not to tell them anything about the murder or the killer. I sat down across the table from Casey and Dell Smith. Casey looked like she'd been punched in the gut, and Dell sat there, his lips tight, the light gone out of his eyes.

"I don't know what Daisy told you…" I said, not sure where to start.

"She said you were able to talk to our daughter," Casey said, hesitation in her voice. "How?"

"I'm a witch. I have the ability to speak to the dead. I stopped when I saw Sheriff Parker's car, and I was lucky enough to meet Sarah's spirit."

There was a way to go about telling someone you had talked to their dead relative, especially if they were fresh to the news that they had lost somebody. It was like walking through a minefield, trying to avoid giving them more grief than they already had.

"Was she in pain?" Casey asked. Dell remained silent.

I took a deep breath. "No. When someone transitions into their spirit form, they no longer feel pain—not on a physical level. Sarah was afraid you'd be mad at her for not coming straight home, but I reassured her that you love her and that you aren't angry."

Casey coughed as tears ran down her cheeks. "I hope she knows we love her—"

"Oh, she does. I reassured her. She knows you love her and she loves you, too. She asked me to make sure that her kitten, Sirius, will be all right."

That produced a response from Dell. I had the feeling he hadn't believed me, and the fact that I knew her kitten's name was the first crack I saw in his demeanor.

"I hate that damned cat. I didn't want it in the first place, but Sarah told us it was the one present she wanted for her birthday and you," he glared at Casey, "had to tell her yes."

Casey paled. "I don't know if we can handle having the cat around now that..." She glanced at Dell and I got an uneasy feeling.

"I'll take him," I said, without a second thought. "I promised Sarah I'd make sure Sirius is looked after." In the back of my mind, I thought that Sarah had known that her father wouldn't want to keep the cat.

Casey again glanced at her husband. "If you would."

"All right. But if I take him, he's *mine*. I'm not giving him back."

"We won't be asking," Dell said. "Did you leave her there in the woods?"

I reassured them that she was all right. "No. Casey, your mother showed up to take Sarah in hand and watch over her. Adele had a message for you—"

"How do we know it was her? How do we know you're not making this up?" Dell said. I immediately sensed that he was one of those humans who didn't like Otherkin.

"Dell, she knows my mother's name—" Casey started to say but he cut her off.

"She could have found that out online," he grumbled.

"Adele thought you might question me," I said. "She asked me to tell Casey this: she always knew it was you who took the ruby ring."

Casey gasped. "Nobody knew about that! I never told anybody, not even Dell."

"Apparently your mother knew," I said. I felt like I was

walking on eggshells. But apparently, Casey believed me enough to relax a little.

"My mother had this beautiful ruby pinkie ring. I loved it but she'd never let me wear it. When I was fourteen, I stole it. She thought she lost it—or at least, she let me believe that. I guess she knew all along but never wanted to call me out on it. You said she's watching over Sarah now?"

"She told me that she's watching out for your whole family, including a daughter named Lila?"

Once again, Dell shifted. He let out a sigh and slumped forward. "Lila? We lost her a year after we were married. She was only two."

"Well, Adele is standing watch over Lila and Sarah, and she's watching over your family. I think she's keeping track of what goes on in the house." I emphasized the latter. I was a little worried about Dell and whether he might take his anger out on Casey. "Anyway, I wanted to let you know that Sarah's okay—she's being cared for. And she misses you."

"She's *not* okay, though, *is she?* She's dead. A butcher ripped her apart," Dell exploded, coming out of his chair. "And no woo-woo crap can bring her back!"

I stumbled back, scrambling out of my chair as he loomed large, looking ready to leap across the table after me. Daisy had stationed Arnie outside the room, who immediately swung in through the open door.

"Is something wrong?" Arnie asked, going from friendly to ever-so-slightly threatening in seconds.

One look at the grim officer and Dell froze, slowly retreating toward his chair.

Casey surprised me. Her tears had stopped and, with a dark glance at her husband, she said, "Deputy? Can you come with us to the house? We need to give Elphyra a kitten and we'd like to make certain that everything goes all right."

Arnie looked confused, but I understood Casey's intent.

Something was off with Dell, and she was also afraid he might do something to the animal before I could collect him.

"She's right," I said. "Can I talk to you a second?" I tapped Arnie on the shoulder as I walked past him, into the hallway. He followed, shutting the door behind him. The moment we were out there, I lowered my voice.

"Listen, Dell's about ready to explode and I think he might hurt Sarah's cat. His wife wants me to take the kitten, and I don't want to chance leaving the animal there. I'm afraid he might try to kill it...or worse."

"I hear you. Give me a minute, and don't go back in there until I return. I can smell the man's anger a mile away."

I glanced at him, curious.

"Didn't you realize? I'm a dog shifter. German shepherd," he said. "Let me go talk to the sheriff." He turned and headed down the hall.

I stood there, waiting outside the conference room where Dell was yelling at his wife. Casey was staring at the table, not saying a word. I suddenly felt sorry for her and wondered if Dell had ever hurt her or the kids. He certainly seemed like a prime candidate for an abuser, although grief could do odd things to people. Maybe it was the loss of his daughter speaking.

Arnie returned before I could speculate any further. "I'll accompany you to their house."

"You might want to check on them now and then—I have a bad feeling about that man," I said. I opened the door.

Dell immediately fell silent.

"Deputy Fryer is going to accompany us to your house so I can pick up Sirius and take him home," I said.

Looking relieved, Casey stood. "Let's go. Dell, are you coming?"

Dell stared at Arnie and me, white-faced. "I need to pick

up something. Can you drive my wife home? I'll be along later."

A wave of thirst washed through the room as Dell wiped his mouth with his hands. A thirst so deep that it was practically screaming.

Casey stared at him for a moment, then—saying nothing —picked up her purse and followed Arnie and me to the door, leaving Dell to sit there in silence.

"You can ride with me, or with Arnie," I said, once we cleared the door.

"You, please. Dell is going to buy booze. I know it." She followed me to my car and, once she fastened her seat belt and I started the car, she broke down, tears running down her face. "Thank you...thank you for telling me my little girl will be all right."

"Of course," I said. "What's your address?"

"231-A Dabob Lane."

After plugging in the directions to the GPS, I pulled out of the parking lot and, followed by Arnie, headed toward her house. It wasn't that far away. They lived in the seedier side of town, where the houses were weathered, rents and mortgages were cheap, and some of the more questionable townsfolk lived.

"I'm glad I could help. Sarah will be okay. And she loves you both," I said, wanting to rest her mind.

"I believe you. Sometimes Dell doesn't process emotion well. And I know him—he'll take Sarah's loss out on the kitten." She hesitated. "Do you mind if I come visit Sirius now and then?"

I wanted to say yes, but I knew better than get involved with someone who wasn't ready to leave their abusive partner. Getting dragged into the middle of their drama, and it *would* happen if I let myself become friends with Casey, wasn't best for my own mental health. Also, it was obvious that Casey wanted contact with *me*—not the cat—because I was the last link she had to her daughter. She'd constantly try to get me to contact Sarah for her, and that wasn't good for the dead. I scrambled for the best answer I could think of.

"You know, it's probably best that you don't, at least not for now. You don't want to make Dell angrier than he already is."

She hung her head. "You're probably right. There," she pointed out the window at a tiny, shabby house. "That's our house."

Arnie accompanied us inside, where Casey found the cat carrier and I tucked Sirius—a scrawny long-haired silver tabby—into the carrier. Casey started to empty his litter box but I told her no, I'd grab a new one on the way home, as well as kitten food. Carrier in hand, I followed her to the door.

"Listen," I said. "I'm probably overstepping my boundaries, especially with the situation now, but if you need to get away, call the sheriff. Daisy's a good cop, and she'll help you find a shelter. If Dell hurts you, leave. Don't stay, thinking it's going to get better." I glanced around. "Do you have any other children?"

Casey shook her head. "No, we lost Lila early and then... after Sarah was born, I had my tubes tied. I could protect her from him, but I didn't want to push my luck. Dell's always had a bad temper, but...I love him."

I love him. Those three little words damned so many women.

As I followed Arnie out into the day, I felt like the morning had dragged on a thousand years. We were nearing the parking lot when his phone rang. He listened for a moment, then turned to me after making sure Casey wasn't within earshot.

"We have him. One of the men called in that he spotted a van matching the description Sarah gave you parked in a rest stop. The license plate matched what she said it was. I'm heading over there. We have to work carefully—we don't have a legal right to search him, so we're going to have to find another way to get him out of the van. Wish us luck, Elphyra."

"All the luck in the world," I said.

CHAPTER TWELVE

AFTER SLIDING THE KITTEN INTO THE BACK SEAT AND fastening the seat belt through the carrier's handle, I drove to the Wisteria Shopping Center, a mini mall on the outside of town. "Here goes nothing," I said to Sirius as I pulled into the parking lot to call Grams. After telling her about my morning, I promised to be home after I found a veterinarian. Before she could say a word, I ended the call and then searched online for a good vet's office. There was one right here in the mini mall, next to a pet store. I called them and asked if they had any appointments open, and to my relief, they did.

I parked in front of the clinic and, with Sirius's carrier in tow, headed inside. I introduced myself and started for the waiting area, but the receptionist stopped me.

"We can take you right in. We had a cancellation this morning."

One of the vet techs led me into an exam room that had another door on the opposite side, an exam table, and a built-in wooden seat. There was also a counter with a sink and cupboards above it. She sat down at a computer terminal.

"Hi, I'm Tara. Let me open a file for you. I need your name, address, and phone number."

"Elphyra MacPherson. That's E-l-p-h-y-r-a, and my last name's spelled M-a-c-P-h-e-r-s-o-n. I live at 7863 Oak Leaf Road, Starlight Hollow WA." From his carrier, Sirius gave a loud mew.

"And your pet's name?"

I hesitated. The name "Sirius" didn't jump out at me, so I said, "Silver, though his collar tag will say 'Sirius,' I think. I don't know if he's microchipped, though I doubt it. I adopted him today. A woman was rehoming him."

"Silver. All right. Do you know how old he is?"

"No, though I think he's still a kitten."

"Well, the doctor should be able to give you an approximate age. Do you know when he was last seen by the vet?"

"My guess is never. Or if so, before she adopted him. Let's put it this way: the cat requires more care and money than she was willing to invest." That wasn't exactly true, but I didn't want to go into the whole mess.

"Okay, the doctor will be in to see you in a moment."

I stopped her. "Before I leave, can I board Silver here for half an hour so I can pick up supplies? This was an impulse decision, and I don't have what I need at home. I can grab everything I need from the pet shop next door—a litter box and food and toys."

"I'm sure we can watch him while you shop for his needs," Tara said.

The door opened and a short, older man with round glasses entered the room. He was bald and had the warmest brown eyes I'd ever seen. He was human, from what I could tell, and was wearing a pair of gray khakis and black leather oxfords. Under his lab coat, he wore a blue and white button-down shirt, and he looked both tidy and tailored, yet moved with a casual ease.

"Well, hello...Elphyra," he said, glancing at the computer screen. "Tara, can you print out the forms and get the file ready while I take a look at our patient here?"

"Of course, Doctor." She pressed a button on the keyboard, then headed out of the room, shutting the door behind her.

"I'm Doctor John. John Stillwater. And who is my patient today?" he asked, peeking into the carrier. "I see we have a kitty."

"I just adopted him. The woman's husband told her to get rid of him, so I decided to give him a home before she did something stupid like dumping him somewhere. I'm renaming him 'Silver,' and I have no clue if he's been fixed, been to a vet, been microchipped, or how old he is."

Doctor John weighed Silver, then palpitated the cat's sides. He took Silver's temperature, murmuring, "Good, we're normal," then opened his mouth and looked at his teeth. After that, Tara returned and she held Silver while Doctor John scanned him for a chip.

"No microchip. He doesn't have fleas, thank goodness, but given what you've told me, we should probably deworm him as a matter of course, and give him his vaccines. Would you like me to microchip him, as well?"

"Yes, please," I said.

The vet tech left, returning with several syringes. The doctor scruffed Silver's fur, then injected him with the usual vaxes and a microchip, then scanned him to confirm it was working.

Afterward, he turned to me. "Do you want to check him for feline leukemia? And we should talk about neutering him. I'd say the little guy's five months old, though he could be a little older and malnourished."

"If he's not neutered, yes, let's set an appointment. And go ahead and do whatever bloodwork on him that you deem necessary. So, five months old? Do you have any idea what breed?"

"Well, you can do a pet DNA test to find out for sure, but by the looks of his paws, he's going to be a big boy. And with the shape of his ears, and the tufty feet and long fur, I think he might have some Maine Coon in him. He could also be part Norwegian Forest cat. He's blue-gray in color, as you can see, and he's growing into what should become a fabulous mane or ruff around his neck. Otherwise, your boy is in good health. He seems laid-back for a kitten that age."

As if to prove him wrong, Silver suddenly jumped, using the doctor's shoulder as a launching pad to catapult him across to the counter with the sink in it. He sat in the sink, staring at the faucet.

"I think he wants the water on?" I asked.

"That would lend toward the Norwegian Forest cat theory," Dr. John said. "Have you ever had a cat?"

"When I was young. I love cats, though. When I saw that he might be headed for a shelter—if he was lucky, or the woods, if he was unlucky—I decided that I had the space and time to devote to a cat. So why not give him a stable life with me? But as I said, it's been a while. What do you recommend I buy?"

"A new collar and tags—even though he's chipped, some people might not think to check for that. Litter box—I recommend avoiding clay litter and scented litters. Litter box scoop, food dish—if you have the choice, get one that's geared to prevent whisker fatigue—"

That led into me asking what "whisker fatigue" was, and when he told me, I immediately thought of Fancypants. Although he was a dragonette, Fancypants also had long whiskers like a cat. I wondered if he grew tired of holding them back to keep them from bending on the edge of a narrow dish.

"You'll also want toys, a scratching post, maybe a cat bed or cat condo. Cats and kittens love to climb. Other than that, keep him indoors. We have too many coyotes around here, and both coyotes and raccoons will attack cats for a meal. We also have bobcats and the occasional puma. Keep his nails trimmed, bring him in for a yearly checkup as well as if you notice a worrisome change in behavior. Love him. Play with him. Maybe get him a friend."

"Good idea. I can do that." In for a penny, in for a pound.

"He'd love having someone who can run zoomies with him, but it's your decision." The doctor filled out several things on the chart. "I have a lab here, so I can take a sample of his blood and by the time you get back from shopping, I'll know if he's clear for feline leukemia."

"Okay, please do. I'll run next door, then return for him—would you prefer me to pay first, or after I come back?"

"After you come back is fine."

I patted Silver on the head. "I'll be back, baby boy. I'm going to get you everything you need." As I left the vet clinic, I realized that I felt happy. Happy like I did when I was around Fancypants. And it hit me—Fancypants needed me. And I needed him. And this was that same feeling. I hadn't been able to save Sarah, but I had been able to rescue her kitten, and that made a tragic day a little bit brighter.

ZOE'S PET UNIVERSE was busy, but not crazy busy. As I shopped for supplies and food—Doctor John had recommended kitten food, given Silver was barely five months old and a little bit malnourished—I came to a corner of the store. There, in a cordoned-off area, was a station set up by the Humane Society. I glanced at the cages against the wall. There were several cats and kittens there, along with a couple of puppies. I opened the gate and walked through, going over to examine the cats.

The woman sitting there gave me a wide smile. She was wearing a nametag that read "Rhonda." "May I help you?"

"Are they all for adoption?"

"Yes," she said. "We're overrun with kittens right now."

I decided that thinking about it was a waste of time. Silver would benefit from a playmate of his kind. "I've adopted a five-month-old boy...he's not fixed yet, though, but I'll be having that done soon. I'd like to get a playmate for him."

"What kind of cats do—" Rhonda started to say but I held up my hand. One cage was calling me, and I walked over to it and peeked in. Inside, a gorgeous little mottled calico sat. She looked about Silver's size.

"Who's this?"

"We're calling her Gem. She's four months old. She's spayed and has had all her vaccines. She gets along well with other cats—in fact, I think she's missing her littermates."

"Can I hold her?"

Rhonda brought Gem out of the cage and handed her to me. She was sleek—with short hair so soft that she felt like a plushie, and a dark mottled pattern in black and orange. She had a white tummy and chest. The minute I took her, she dove beneath my chin and dug into my shirt. She trembled and, for some reason that made me want to cry. I looked down at her, pressed against my chest, and my heart melted.

"I'll take her. She's going home with me today." That was it. In a split second—less time than it took to blink—I was in love.

"She's litter box-trained, and she's in good health. I'll get the forms." Rhonda looked relieved. "I'm glad you're taking her. She's been standoffish with everybody else who looked at her and several potential adopters said she's too shy."

I held the kitten up as I stared into her eyes. I gave her the slow blink that said *I love you.* "You want to come home with me?"

As if in answer, Gem squirmed, trying to get back under my chin. I shushed her—she was mewing. "It's all right. You're going home with me. But I have to fill out some forms first." I looked over at the Rhonda. "I'll need a carrier. And I need to call the vet next door and let them know I'll be a few more minutes."

As she set Gem back in the cage, the kitten started to meow loudly. "I think you've made a friend," Rhonda said.

I called the vet and asked them to wait a couple minutes —that I had picked out a friend for Silver. They said Silver had checked out negative for feline leukemia so we were good to go. I asked if they had another slot open and they said to bring Gem in and they'd give her an exam.

I filled out the forms, paid the adoption fee, and bought all the supplies—after doubling the food dishes, cat beds, and adding the carrier. Rhonda set Gem into the carrier and the kitten quieted right down, as if she knew that I wasn't abandoning her.

I took her back to the vet and Doctor John checked her out. Gem meowed the entire time.

"You have a set of healthy lungs on you," he said, grinning. "She's in good shape. She's about ten weeks old—four and a half months. She's at a good age to play with Silver. He's underweight, so by the time he catches up to what he should be, she'll be old enough to hold her own." He paused, then said, "Congratulations on your new family members. Will your husband mind?"

Instinctively I knew he wasn't trying to make a pass. He was concerned that perhaps I hadn't consulted anybody else who lived with me.

"I'm not married, and I don't have kids. So, there's

nobody to mind except my dragonette. And he's friendly and would love playmates, I think."

"A dragonette? I'd love to meet him some time. I've heard of them, but have never seen one. Will *he* be safe around *them*?" Doctor John asked with a laugh.

I snickered. "By the time they're adults, they'll be twice as big as he is. He's little. And he's quite intelligent. Everything will be fine."

Doctor John looked relieved. He carried the two carriers out to the waiting room for me, where I paid the bill. Then, carriers firmly locked in the backseat, I fastened my seat belt and—with my new family members both wailing like toddlers —headed for home.

GRAMS WAS IN THE SHOP, but the parking lot was empty and when she heard me pull in, she came out of the store and walked over to the car. I hopped out of the driver's seat and opened the back door.

"Help me carry things inside?" I asked.

She stared at the carriers and started to laugh. "I wondered how long you'd last without cats. Your father loved them. I wish your mother did."

"We had a cat when I was younger and I adored her, I remember. Zeisal was a tortie like Gem, and my father found when I was three. She died when I was fifteen and I was heartbroken. In fact, she looked like Gem." It suddenly hit me—the way Gem had clung to me felt the same way as when Zeisal had cuddled against me. *Exactly* the same. "I wonder..."

As we placed the carriers in the living room and then brought in all the supplies, Fancypants came winging in. He made a beeline for the carriers and clapped his hands.

"Friends! You brought home friends!"

"You like cats?" I asked.

"Dragonettes are the cats of the dragon realm," he said.

"I can see the similarities. Now be careful with them, they're both babies," I warned him. But the look on his face reassured me there would be no problems. Fancypants was smitten.

"I'll help you take care of them and I can watch them if you're busy," he said, hopping from the top of one carrier to the other. "Can you bring them out now? Should I give them some of the muffin I was eating?"

"Cats are obligate carnivores. They're better off with grain-free cat food. I don't want to get them started eating people food," I said. "So, you enjoy that muffin all by yourself. Grams, do you mind setting up the litter boxes? One can go in the hall bath, and the other...well...by the washer and dryer, I guess. I'll get their food and water dishes ready. For the first day or so, let's confine them to the hall bathroom so I can kitten-proof the house."

I found a tray in the kitchen and put food and water out, setting them in the hall bath. I'd bought the whisker-fatigue dishes, and they did seem like they'd be much easier on the cats. Making sure the toilet seat was down, I set a large cat bed in the walk-in shower—that would be easy enough for them to find, and then scattered a couple toys on the floor.

Grams and I, and—of course, Fancypants—took them into the bathroom and we sat on the floor and opened the carriers. I found myself grateful that the bath wasn't tiny—it wasn't huge, either, but it was a good-enough size to give them a bit of room.

"Now that we have a chance to sit and talk, where on earth did you find them?" Gram asked. She was sitting cross-legged, wearing a pair of walking shorts and a light blouse. For being over a hundred, she looked good. She looked about middle-aged, and while her skin had lost the tone of youth, I could still see the muscle definition.

I leaned back against the wall, watching Gem and Silver as they set out to explore their new surroundings. "I had quite the morning." I proceeded to tell her about the murder, and Sarah's ghost, and the way her parents had acted. "I didn't trust the father. I had the uneasy feeling he was either going to dump Silver—Sirius was his name but I changed it—or kill the kitten. I think Sarah's mother felt the same way because the minute I suggested taking the kitten, she was all over it."

"They're going to be divorced in a year, mark my words. Tragedy either brings people together, or it tears them apart." Grams shook her head. "When your grandfather died, Peter and I pulled together as a team. We took the grief and shared it, and it strengthened our marriage. It's always a bitter branch. In an ideal world, a parent shouldn't outlive their child, but it happens all the time, and it's a tragedy that few talk about openly."

Gem clambered up on my lap, then up my shirt to where she was clinging to me again. I nuzzled her.

"Gem reminds me of Zeisal, in so many ways. But mostly in the feeling I have when I'm holding her." I teared up. "When I lost Zeisal, I lost the love of my life—that pure, unadulterated love that bonds two beings together without any conditions. When I lost Rian, I lost love again, in a different way." As tears trailed down my cheek, Gem stood with her paws on my shoulders and licked them away.

"You two have been around the Wheel before," Grams said. "She found you again."

"Zeisal?" I asked, afraid to voice what I had been hoping.

"Yes, I believe so. But remember: she's different this time. She's not the same cat that she was. Let her be who she needs to be this lifetime. She has a different mission. Don't try to force her into the vision you remember." Grams picked up Silver. "And who are you, little boy?"

He mewed but quickly settled down on her lap, purring himself to sleep as she petted him.

"It's been a while since I've slowed down enough to sit silently with an animal," she said. "It's calming."

"Yeah, I agree." I nuzzled Gem, then realized she'd fallen asleep on my chest. "So, Zeisal's come back to me. I've missed her. There's something so unconditional about their love. Animals are honest. They never lie to you."

"You never had a dog, did you?"

"No," I said. "I like dogs, but... This is hard to explain. They're so forgiving. They accept abuse because that's who they are—loyal to the death. They try to please their owners to a point that it breaks my heart. Nobody, person or animal, should stay with an abuser. My loyalty will *always* be conditional. A cat will lash out if you hurt it, if it can. And I like that. I like being held accountable." I paused, then looked over at Grams. "I'm ready for the cord cutting ceremony. Can we do it now?"

"Yes, we can. But did you want Bree here?"

"No, she's dealing with her own crisis right now—the stalker, you know."

"All right. Shall we go outside in the garden?"

I thought about it. "Yeah, that's a good place."

"Let's let this pair rest and get acquainted."

"Do you think they'll be okay together?" I started to say, but as we stood, gently placing the kittens in the cat bed, they shifted, finding each other, and quickly curled together in a ball of fluff and razorblades. Silver squinted, opening one eye, and he leaned over, licking Gem's head. A few moments later, they were both snoozing.

"Yes, I think they'll be fine," Grams said. "Come on, let's

gather a few things and head outside. It's time for you to let go of the past, my dear."

Knowing she was right, even though a part of my past I thought long gone had reached out to return to me, I followed her out of the bathroom and softly closed the door.

CHAPTER THIRTEEN

IT WAS TWO FORTY-FIVE, SO I DIDN'T BOTHER PUTTING A note on my store. Apparently, the gods knew that I needed the time today and had steered potential customers away. Grams and I gathered our gear and changed into our ritual regalia, then found a place near one of the rose bushes, where she had me sit down on a blanket. Usually I didn't care for the sun, but today was different. Everything felt surreal, like I'd smoked way too much weed.

"I feel like I'm high," I said. I was wearing a long gown, not exactly Grecian, that draped down to my ankles with a slit on both sides that showed my upper thighs. Sleeveless, it was a summer ritual dress. My tattoos showed, the sleeves on my forearms brilliant and magical in themselves.

Grams was in a black gown that was fitted at the waist. The skirt was gauzy, the hemline fluttering in the wind. She had drawn a circle on the ground with her dagger, and in the center of the circle was a flowerpot filled with soil. A blade stood in the planter, the tip buried deep in the pot. Tied to the hilt was a ruby ribbon, plaited, with a nine-foot length ending by our feet.

"The magical energy is strong," Fancypants said. He swiveled his neck to stare at Grams. "I can feel the energy flowing off you."

Grams stood in front of the flowerpot and held out her dagger. I closed my eyes, sinking into the energy. Even Fancypants quieted down, watching somberly. Grams walked the circle as she cast the magic.

> *Once around, I draw this ring, a world sacred, a world between.*
> *Twice around, I draw this space, with the gods, face to face.*
> *Thrice around, this circle I seal, let now the spirit realm reveal.*

I felt the energy settle around us, thick and sparkling. It washed through the circle, and every ache and pain I felt was washed away. I leaned back, resting my hands behind me on the grass. Suddenly, it was as though I could breathe again.

Grams set down her dagger and walked over to sit down in front of me. She picked up the end of the ribbon and handed it to me. I stared at it. Once I took hold, there was no going back. Initiating magical action meant either follow-through or letting energy go awry, and the last thing I wanted to do was let cord cutting energy go askew. It could cut off anybody if it wasn't focused, and the last thing I wanted to do was lose a friend.

"Do you want to go through with it?" Grams said. "I won't push you. If you aren't ready, say so and we'll devoke the circle and leave it be."

I thought about it. Rian had come to me, asking me to let him go. He wanted me to get on with my life, to be happy. I didn't want to forcibly keep him bound to this plane. That was cruel. And...I needed to get out of the mire. I needed to be brave and face my future instead of hiding from it. I slowly reached out, then opened my hand.

"I'm ready," I said, swallowing hard.

"Don't suppress your fear—don't suppress your sorrow. You need to walk through the fire to let it go." She placed the ribbon in my hand, and I could feel Rian's essence embodied in the red satin. I had my own dagger with me, sitting on the ground beside me.

"What now?" I asked.

"I want you to talk to Rian. To tell him you're ready to move forward. Tell him how you loved him, that you'll always love him but that you have to move into the present and leave him in the past. While you're talking, unravel the braid all the way to the knot around the sword. Then, when you have finished, tell him goodbye, consign him to the Veil, and use your dagger to cut through the ribbons, which we'll burn in the firepit. After that, you're not to talk about Rian for a month. Every time you utter his name, you draw him back. After a month, the pain of cutting the cords will lessen enough that you can begin to speak about him again."

Grams knelt behind the flower pot, her hands flat against the earth. "I'm grounding the circle, grounding us in the present."

I stared at the ribbons in my hand, then stood. As I untangled the braid, I took a deep breath and licked my lips. I'd already said everything there was to say, time and again.

"Rian, I'm ready to let you go. You asked me to let your spirit fly free, and I'm here to honor that request. It's so hard, because I still feel guilt. I survived, and you didn't." I paused, then unwound another section of the ribbons. "Logically, I know it's not my fault, and I know you don't blame me. But I still blame myself, and I know that it's time to stop. Clinging to the dreams of what we were going to do won't help either one of us."

I stopped, realizing that I was crying. "Damn it, why did you die? Why did you..." I wanted to scream, to ask why he destroyed our future. But he hadn't done anything wrong.

"Get angry at the right person," Grams said. "Why are you so afraid to be angry at the vampire who did this?"

I gasped. "Because I should have known. I shouldn't have gotten drunk that night—"

"Rian was drunk, too. Both of you were. But neither one of you was to blame. People make mistakes. You and Rian made a mistake, and you paid dearly. But he didn't ask to be murdered, and you didn't lead him into it."

A final stone, lodged deep in my heart, broke loose. It crumbled and I began to sob. "I have to let you go. I can't carry this weight any longer. It's so heavy, and it's dragging every thought, everything I do, down into the grave with you."

I stared at the ribbon. It was fully unwound.

"Rian, I love you. I'll always love you, but I have to leave you in the past. You're no longer part of my life, but you'll always be in my heart. Go, be free, do what you need to do. I let you go. I let your spirit fly—and maybe, if it's meant to be, we'll find each other again in another life."

And then, before I could change my mind, I lifted my dagger with my right hand. Holding the cords in my left, I severed the link between us.

As the ribbons fell to the ground, I stared at the dagger in the plant potter. It was done. I could feel a soft sigh, and as I looked up, I saw Rian standing there, a look of relief and love on his face. *Thank you*, he said, as he faded. *I'll always love you.*

I raised my hand, watching as he vanished, my tears vanishing with him. I was cried out. There would still be tears to come, but for now, the well was dry. The future suddenly felt vast with possibilities. I knelt by the rose bush nearest me and buried my nose in a bloom. Fancypants landed on my shoulder, and he awkwardly patted my hair. Grams walked over to the planter, and she picked up all the ribbons.

In silence, we carried them to the firepit and she tossed them in, along with a little fire starter, and handed me the matches. Still silent, I lit the match and dropped it atop the ribbons. As they burned, ashes flickering into the sky, I realized that I had let go of a major part of my life. And now... now what would happen?

AT SIX, Grams decided to take a nap. She peeked into the hall bath where I was playing with the kittens. "I'll eat dinner when I get up. You go ahead and do whatever you like—don't fret about me."

I kissed her on the cheek. I was about to text Bree, to tell her about the day, when my phone rang. It was Daisy. Worried that there had been another murder, I answered.

"Elphyra? Are you busy?"

I sighed. "Not really, but I don't think I can try to talk to another spirit right now, if there's been another murder. I'm exhausted—"

"No, no...that's not why I'm calling." She paused, then said, "We caught the killer, thanks to the information that Sarah gave you."

My heart jumped a beat. "You *did*? And you're sure it's him?"

"Yeah, we found all the evidence we needed. But..."

"There's a but?" *Please, don't let him get off on a technicality*, I thought.

"Probably not what you're thinking. I guess Sarah's father was listening in on a police scanner or something. We're not sure. When we arrived at the police station with the suspect, Dell was waiting, hiding behind the big sign in front. As we walked the suspect toward the doors, Dell shot him. Killed him dead."

I gasped. "Dell *killed* the serial killer?"

To be honest, though I was shocked, I was also relieved. It would save the county a huge amount in court fees and prevent him from ever escaping or being released back into the populace. But I didn't want to say that aloud, and also— Dell could have made a mistake and shot someone else by mistake.

"Yeah. We're positive he was the killer. We found souvenirs in his possession from each kill. We identified him as Heinrich Stephenson, going by the name Joe Gregor. He's a rogue shifter who was abandoned when he was a child. He's not like most wolf shifters. He doesn't turn into a wolf when he shifts. He's actually one of the rare true lycanthropes. He shifts into a monster between human and wolf."

I froze. "Lycanthrope? Werewolf, you mean? I didn't know that was an actual thing. I thought it was some scary story shifter-haters used to stir up trouble."

"Oh, it's a real thing, all right. Lycanthropes are danger-ous. They're sterile themselves, but they're a genetic muta-tion, born to wolf shifters in about one in five thousand instances. They usually live outside the cities and are most often nomadic. We are checking into his background now. But at least we caught him, thanks to you and to Sarah. I wanted you to know."

I thanked her and, seeing that the kittens were down for a nap, I wandered into the living room, shutting the door behind me. Fancypants was on the coffee table, playing a slide puzzle game on my tablet.

"So, they caught the killer," I said.

The dragonette looked over at me. "That's a good thing, right?"

"Yeah, it is," I said, deciding to leave it at that. "What do you want for dinner?"

"I don't care," he said, absorbed in the game.

In the kitchen, I poked through the fridge until I found a frozen pizza. I unwrapped it and placed it on a baking sheet, and then put it in the oven. Then, while I waited for it to bake, I called Bree.

"How's it going?"

"I sure appreciate having Faron's people being around as guards. I feel safe. I hate not feeling like I can take care of myself."

I told her what had happened through the day, from Sarah's ghost, to the cord cutting ritual, to Daisy catching the killer, to Dell assassinating him. "I feel like I've been through the wringer, Bree."

"That's a lot to take in. Are you okay?"

Rather than automatically respond, I thought about her question for a moment. "I think so. I'm exhausted. I wish I could unsee so many things. But the cord cutting, while hard, was necessary."

"Your great-grandmother is a gem."

"Yes, she is. Oh! I didn't tell you, speaking of gems. I brought home Sarah's kitten, along with a playmate." I told her about Gem and Silver, until the doorbell rang. "Someone's here. I'll call you back in a while."

I answered the door to find Faron standing there. He leaned against the door post, wearing a pair of leather pants and a low V-neck sweater. His hair was loose, flowing over his shoulders, a rich cascade of brunet waves. He had a scruff of a beard, and his eyes sparkled.

Suddenly, I felt shy and I realized it was because now, I couldn't use Rian as an excuse. Cutting the cords forced me to be honest with my decisions. If I was interested, I couldn't stand behind his memory and use it as a barrier. If

I decided I didn't want to get involved, I had to be upfront and honest and—again—not use Rian as an excuse.

"You look wiped," Faron said. "What happened? I've been in meetings all day." He reached out and stroked my cheek, ending with a finger running across my lips.

"I am. Grams is asleep, I don't want to bother her. Come in. I have a pizza ready to come out of the oven and I'm starved. You hungry?"

"That sounds good, if you have enough—" He paused as he entered the house. "What's this? I smell cat."

"That's because I now am the mother to two cats. You might say I inherited one and adopted the other for a play-mate." I took the pizza out of the oven as Faron opened the cupboard and took out two plates. "Fancypants needs his plate, too. He hasn't eaten yet."

"Whoops! Can't have that," Faron said. "You going to introduce me to your pussies?" he asked, grinning.

I gave him the side-eye. "Dude..."

"*Pussy cats! Kittens!*" He laughed, but I could feel his desire. He hadn't dressed up for *himself* tonight.

"Later. For now, food." I cut up a slice of pizza for Fancy-pants and moved his high chair to the table. He had been sitting on the counter, waiting patiently, and now he flew over and settled into the chair, tying his bib around his neck. It had been his idea. Fancypants was a little prim and proper—far more fastidious than I was.

"Here, can you give this to Fancypants?" I handed the plate to Faron.

He set the plate in front of the dragonette. "Here you go. Do you use silverware?"

Fancypants coiled his neck, then let out a laugh. "No, thank you, Sir Wolf. I'm not dexterous enough to handle a fork. But if you could hand me a napkin, I'd appreciate it."

Faron glanced at me and winked, then picked up a napkin and handed it to Fancypants. "Here you go."

I carried the pizza to the table, setting the pan in the center. Faron handed me a plate and then sat down opposite. As I loaded a slice of the meat lover's pizza with parmesan, my back grumbled and my neck ached. I suddenly realized my energy reserves were dipping into the negatives.

"I'm so tired," I said.

"What happened today?" Faron asked, biting into his slice.

I swallowed, focusing on the mouth feel of tomato sauce and cheese and salty pepperoni, ham, and sausage. "Mmm," I said, letting the tastes mingle together, then slide down my throat. "I need this. I need the food, I need to sit and relax, I need to just...be."

"Rough day, then?" Faron glanced at my plate and slid another slice of pizza onto it. "You're done with the first. Eat up. Do you want something to drink?"

"I'd love a cognac," I said. "I don't drink often, but right now I think I want one."

"Do you have any booze in the house?" Faron asked. "Tell me where and I'll get you a drink."

"There's a liquor cabinet in the living room. I have a few bottles of liquor in there."

He gave me an odd look, then ducked out of the kitchen. When he returned, he had two cordial glasses filled with an amber liquid. He handed me one and I took a sip.

"Wow, it's been a while since I've had a drink," I said, shivering as the brandy raced down my throat, warming me inside and out.

"Do you mind if I ask why?" Faron asked.

I paused, then said, "I've never been much of a drinker, but the night...when the vampire caught us, we were tipsy and we weren't alert as to what was going on around us. We were too drunk to get away." I stared into my glass. "I think I'm afraid of losing control."

"That makes sense. Well, you don't have to drink if you don't want to. There's no rule saying you must. It's more social than anything else." He tasted the brandy. "That's a good brandy, though. It's meant for leisurely sipping." He hesitated, then said, "Not to bring up a sensitive subject, but I heard about the serial killer today. He was shot while being hauled into the station. You know about that, don't you?"

"I know more than I want to know." I told him what had transpired that morning as we finished our dinner. As I carried my dish to the sink, Faron got up to help me. "Do you usually help out with meals at home?" I asked. I suddenly realized I'd never been to his house and I had no idea what the commune was like.

"You'd be surprised what I help out with," he said. "Am I King of our Pack? Yes. Does this excuse me from jumping in to help? No. Everybody pulls their own weight in the commune, and those who can't—the infants, the disabled—we all look after them. The children have their chores. And the elderly watch over the young ones and teach the old traditions to make sure they're passed down."

I nodded. "It sounds very community oriented."

"We're a Pack, not a group of individualists. Oh, we all have our own talents, but we're group-minded." He picked up a dish towel and dried the dishes as I washed them. There weren't enough to stack in the dishwasher.

Fancypants hovered near us for a moment. "I'm going to my meeting," he said.

"Meeting?" Faron eyed him curiously.

"Yeah," the dragonette said, flying out of the room.

"Now he's taking meetings?" Faron asked me, the hint of a grin on his lips.

I motioned for him to follow me into the living room,

where I turned on the computer and set it up so that Fancypants could talk through a microphone. I brought up the website and made certain everything was working.

"Fancypants discovered an online group of dragonettes who chat once a week. They're all bonded, and it's one way to allay their sense of isolation from their own kind. Rather odd, given most of the dragonettes don't get together in the wild, but I guess it comes from living with people who are, for all intents and purposes, pack animals."

"That's all very interesting," he said, sounding like it was the last thing in the world he wanted to talk about. "Elphyra…"

I glanced at him. "Yes?"

"I want you to get to know my Pack. I want you to understand what it's like to be a part of a community like mine." His voice dropped as he moved toward me.

"Why?" I asked.

"Someday, you might have reason to live with us," he said, moving closer. He took me in his arms and lowered his lips to brush mine. "I want you to understand my world."

I trembled, then took his hand and led him back to the kitchen.

"Show me," I whispered, leaning up to kiss him again. My body trembled. The chemistry between us was undeniable and I pressed against him, my breasts against his chest, my hips against his. I could feel him, beneath his jeans, hard and hungry.

"Are you sure?" he asked, coming up for air. "Your Grams…"

"Is asleep. But follow me." I led him out the kitchen door, guiding him under the evening sky to a mossy spot by the herb garden. I pulled him close again, taking his hand and placing it on my hip. "It's time. I want you. I *need* you. I'm so hungry for your touch. It's been so long. Feel me. Take me down, ride me hard."

And then, we were in a scramble, stripping off clothes, till we stood there naked under the twilight sky. I stood back, looking at him. His skin was smooth and taut. He had just the right amount of hair, sprinkled across his chest, leading to the V above his waist. And he was hard—his cock long and pink and throbbing, pulsating as he feasted his gaze on me.

I reached out and ran my finger along his penis, grasping around the root as I fell to my knees and brought him to my mouth. Faron moaned, his hands on my shoulders, and arched back as I pursed my lips around the head and slowly sucked him into my mouth, tightening my lips to form as much suction as possible.

"Elphyra...oh you're good, don't stop," he said, his breath jagged as his glutes tightened and he thrust forward, deeper into my mouth. He smelled like musk, pure animal hunger, and my nipples stiffened under the cool evening air. I was wet, slippery, and I wanted him in me. I doubled down, bobbing my head along his shaft, moaning as he filled my mouth with his girth and length.

Before he could come, he pulled away. His eyes gleamed with a feral light as he grabbed me around the waist and sought my mouth. He kissed me, his hands exploring my body in a frenzy of lust. He slid one hand between my legs, feeling for my clit, and rubbed—slowly at first, then with more insistence, swirling his fingers. I let out another cry as he lowered me to the ground and I spread my legs for him, welcoming him in.

Faron hovered above me, then instead of entering me, he slid down my body, leaving a trail of kisses on my breasts, my stomach, my lower abs. When he came to the center between my thighs, he took hold of my waist and lowered his mouth to my clit, sucking and nibbling, driving me wild as I squirmed. I wanted him to continue, and yet I wanted him in me.

"More, more..." I said, trying to breathe. I held his head between my legs, reveling in the feel of his tongue on me, urging me to let go of control. It had been so long since I'd felt a man touch me this way, over a year. Rian had been more reticent about sex. It had been *good*, but it had never quite been tear-your-clothes-off good. But Faron, he knew how to use his tongue, and his fingers.

He sucked harder and I still resisted letting go of that final piece of control. But he refused to stop, and I couldn't hold on any longer. I bucked against him, my hips driving upward, and then I shrieked, all the pain and anger came rushing out, the hunger for touch, the year of repression—it all burst out in one long, pulsating orgasm that shook me to the core.

Tears raced down my cheeks, but instead of waiting, Faron crawled up and, after quickly donning a condom, slid inside me, once again taking control of the situation. I tried to fight, tried find some foundation on which to stand, but the feel of him entering me, the feel of his cock lodged deep within me as he rode me, hips grinding, driving me on. Another shockwave hit, and yet another, and they kept coming—little quakes that shook everything I thought I remembered.

The string of orgasms hit me, rippling through me as they unleashed the hunger I'd stored away during the past year, and I let out a single high-pitched scream, then collapsed as he came with a muffled growl. As his cock continued to pulse inside me, I curled in his arms, and he murmured to me, soft words that I couldn't understand. A moment later, as we settled, he kissed me. We lay there in silence for a few minutes, the air cool against our flesh, and then Faron stirred.

"Are you ready for more?" he asked, his voice gentle. Once

again, he took me—gently this time—and we made love under the growing stars.

WE FINISHED DRESSING and were headed inside, intending to take a shower, when my phone rang and I picked up.

Bree sounded frantic. "Do you know where Faron is?"

"He's right here." I handed the phone to him. "It's Bree."

"Hey, Bree, what's up? Really? They should be there by now... All right, I'll be over in a few minutes... No, don't feel bad," he added, handing me back the phone. "I asked Hans and Paris to stand watch tonight but they haven't shown up. Lief and Claudette had to leave. I'm going to go over there. Want to come with me?"

As exhausted and satiated as I was, sitting out under the stars keeping watch on Bree's house sounded like a calm end to an eventful day.

"We can shower later. Let me change clothes and grab a light jacket. It's cooling off tonight." I darted into my bedroom and quickly changed clothes. I smelled like Faron. He smelled safe, and warm.

For now, though, I found an oversized fleece throw and a waterproof pillow and scribbled a note to Grams. I cracked her door to make certain all was well—she was getting up there, after all. The soft sound of her snoring reassured me, so I taped the note to her door.

Once back in the living room, I pulled on a pair of flat boots that were both comfortable and waterproof, grabbing a light jacket just in case, and told Fancypants I didn't know when I'd be home. "I'll have my phone, but tell Grams to text instead of call. If we end up staying later, I don't want any ringing to give us away, in case Bree's stalker shows up. I'll put the phone on vibrate."

"I checked with Merry," Faron said. "She and Lyle had a flat tire, and they're in the middle of changing it, and they didn't have Bree's number to tell her. They don't have a spare, so they have to wait for someone from the Pack to reach them. And she thinks she's getting the stomach flu. I told them to go home. They're married and if she's sick, it's likely that Lyle will come down with it too."

"I'll stay with you. I could use a night out under the stars." I showed him the blanket and pillow. "I come prepared."

He stopped for a moment, smiling. "I'd like that. We'll stop on the way and get coffee," Faron said, taking the blanket and pillow from me. "I'll toss these in the back of the truck." He paused again, then asked. "Are you all right? I hope I didn't push you—"

"I'm good," I said, meaning it. "I needed that. I needed *you*. We can talk about it later, but I have no regrets."

"I'm glad to know that, because neither do I," Faron said.

Fancypants waved us off as we headed out the door. "Behave!"

I laughed. "I wouldn't do anything else," I said, closing the door behind us.

CHAPTER FOURTEEN

WE WERE CLIMBING INTO THE TRUCK WHEN A VOICE
called out, "Hey, you headed out?"

I whirled to see Bran standing there. He was in a pair of
low-cut jeans, his belt riding low on his hips over the T-shirt
he was wearing. His hair was up in a manbun, and he looked
more ripped than usual.

Feeling awkward, wondering if he could smell the sex on
us, I said, "We're headed over to Bree's. Long story short,
we're watching over her property because of that stalker. The
cops can't be there all the time, and he's escalated his
behavior."

Bran's smile immediately vanished. "You want some help?"

I wanted to say no, and yet—truth was, we weren't headed
over to Bree's for a makeout party. This was serious business.
I glanced at Faron.

His eyes narrowing, Faron hesitated, then he said, "Sure.
You'll have to ride in the back of the truck, though."

Bran looked at me again, then jumped over the tailgate,
into the back of the truck. I tossed him my blanket and

pillow, and he settled down, wrapping the blanket around him.

"This is cozy."

"Right," Faron said. He yanked open the passenger door for me. "Get in. We don't want to leave her alone there for long. That perv could easily be watching, especially if he realizes her house is under surveillance."

As I fastened my seat belt, I felt like we were in the proverbial "Two's company but three's a crowd" scenario. But I wasn't Jack, and Faron and Bran weren't Janet and Chrissy.

Faron glanced at me. "Did you mind if he comes along?"

"No, we can use the help," I said, avoiding looking into the rearview mirror. "I didn't invite him—I want you to know that." I paused, then groaned. "I wonder if Grams invited him earlier."

"Your great-grandmother really prefers him over me?" Faron asked, shifting gears as we turned at the end of the drive onto the street.

"He's a witch. That makes all the difference to her," I said.

"What about to you? I know you find him attractive." He bit into his words, and I could tell he was trying to control his temper.

"*You're* the one I just had sex with. It's true, Bran's attractive and he cares about people. But the same goes for you. It would be easier if one of you was a real asshole. Like I *thought* you were when I first met you. But tonight was special, Faron. I needed the release, and I'm grateful that you were the one to help me find my way. It was so good—*you* were so good."

Faron gave me a grunt, but it sounded halfway civil. "At least you're honest," he said.

"I don't lie. Neither you nor Bran deserve a lie. I won't do that to people," I said. I was about to say that Rian and I had based our relationship on honesty, but then I thought about the cord cutting and remembered I wasn't to bring up his name. "It's served me well in the past, and I intend to keep it that way."

"Thank you," Faron said gruffly. "Whatever happens, at least I know you won't lead me on as a game. And what I felt back there was real, woman, so you know."

"For me, too." I glanced at the back window. Bran was seated in a meditation pose, and I wondered how he could manage any form of meditation given the bumpy ride. We arrived at Bree's house, and I hurried out of the truck.

"It's us, we're here," I called as I rang the bell. A moment later, I heard the locks turn and Bree peeked out. She stood back, opening the door.

"Thank you for coming. I didn't realize how on edge I've been until Lief and Claudette went home." She sat down on the edge of the sofa. "I can't go on this way. I can't rely on bodyguards forever. What if we never find him?"

"We will," Faron said. "In fact, I had an idea on the way over. I think we should leave—ostensibly—and then sneak back. If he thinks you're alone, he might make a move and then we can catch him. We need to lay the trap."

Bree let out a shaky sigh. "That sounds like a plan, as scared as it makes me. I've never felt this vulnerable before and I never want to feel this way again."

"What do we do?" I asked.

"We make a big show of leaving, then we park a few blocks away, and walk back through the alleys and back streets."

Unlike some of the cities, Starlight Hollow still was a grid of streets and alleys. It was possible to traverse a good share of the town through the alleyways, keeping away from the main view of the street. If Bree's stalker was watching, he was probably hiding out either across the street in the vacant lot, or he was back in the graveyard. The house to her right was occupied by an older couple, and they were always home.

Across the street, the lot was vacant, but the houses to either side were occupied. And, of course, to the left of Bree's property was the graveyard.

"Where will we hide?" Bran asked. "Maybe we should split up—one of us take the backyard, and the other two, hide near the graveyard, to the side of the house." He paused, looking directly at me. "I'll take the backyard," he said, and I could hear a hundred thoughts tucked into that one sentence.

I met his gaze. He stared at me, open and unarmed, honest and understanding, and I wondered if he had heard me talking in the truck.

Faron read the same thing into his words as I did. "Thanks, old chap," he said.

"I'm not British and neither are you," Bran said, but he laughed. "All right, let's say a loud farewell. Make sure you're heard."

I gave Bree a hug. "Maybe this will work," I said.

"Maybe it will." She hugged me tight. "Thanks...for everything."

I held tight to her hands before I let go. "We'll find him. I promise you that."

WE WERE ON THE PORCH, chatting loudly.

"I wish we could stay," I said, "but we promised Grams we'd be back for a late supper."

"I wish you could stay, too," Bree said. "Give her and May my love!"

"I'll make sure my men can get here tomorrow morning. I'm sorry plans got fucked up tonight," Faron said.

As Bree waved us off, we headed for the truck. Now that our plan was in motion, I wasn't too thrilled about it. We were leaving her alone, and although it was only for fifteen minutes or so, that could be all the stalker needed. But for the lack of a better plan—and without Daisy's help —this was the best option. We couldn't stake out her house every single night from now until the stalker tripped himself up.

As we drove away, I held my arms tight against my stomach.

Faron noticed. "Are you okay?"

"I'm nervous. After the crap I've seen with the serial killer, this scares the fuck out of me. Remember, I ended up seeing a couple of the bodies. And after what I've been through the past year or so, part of me wants to lock Bree in an ivory tower and throw away the key. I can't let anything bad happen to my best friend."

"I understand, I really do. But we won't let it come to that. This whole maneuver tonight is to attempt a capture. My gut tells me he'll come in if he thinks she's unprotected. He won't want to wait until we're back again with rein-forcements."

"I trust you," I said. "I hope that this works."

We parked about a block and a half away from Bree's house, in a turnout where hopefully we wouldn't be noticed. At least we didn't have to worry about the serial killer anymore. I shrugged on the light jacket I'd added at the last minute and slipped out of the car. Bran and Faron joined me, flanking both sides. Their auras were both in check, and for now—at least—they had quashed their rivalry.

"Where do we go now?" I asked.

"We'll cut through the alleys till we reach Bree's house, then Bran will take the backyard and we'll monitor the grave-yard next door." Faron glanced at Bran.

"I didn't expect to be doing this, so I didn't bring any weapons." I had left the switchblade Grams had given me at home, not even thinking to bring it.

"No problem, I'm a black belt in several martial arts specialties," Bran said.

Faron let out a low whistle. "Well, that's good to know. I can brawl with the best of them. And since I'm a shifter, my strength..."

"Is worth two of me," Bran said. "That's gotta help. In wolf form, is your bite worse than your bark?" As we walked below the streetlamps, he grinned, probably to show that he wasn't taking a cheap shot.

"Seriously? Wolf shifters, when in our alt-forms, are stronger than the animals we become, too. So, teeth stronger, jaws stronger, *everything's*...stronger." He paused, glancing at me.

I blushed, trying to keep my mind from wandering.

Over the years, I had known some women who slept with their shifter lovers while the men were in alt-form, but that was a little too close to bestiality to me. If it had been in lycanthrope form—more human than beast but still monstrous—I would have an easier time accepting it, though that felt kinky as hell. It wasn't that I didn't enjoy a good throwdown with blindfold and restraints, but...

Quit thinking about sex, I scolded myself, realizing I wanted more. Fucking Faron had been a drop in the ocean and I was thirsty as all get out. *That's not what tonight's about.*

Faron shifted, glancing at me. I caught my breath. He winked at me, then flicked the tip of his tongue through his teeth. He must be able to read my scent. And if my scent had shifted with my thoughts...then he knew I wanted him again. I hesitantly reached out and took his hand, squeezing it, then quickly let go.

Quietly we slipped through the alleys, behind the homes where families were settling in for the night, where kids were whining about taking baths and going to bed, couples were either watching TV or making love or fighting, where the business of life was taking place.

Here and there a dog barked, cats leapt on the fences to stare at us, and behind one house we saw a coyote who slunk off into the night. I suddenly felt alien, as though I were looking in on what it meant to be human—what it meant to be an observer instead of participating in the great parade of existence. I'd experienced this before, but it had been a while. Usually, it was while I was driving at night on a highway, alone in my car with the music going and the rain pouring.

We neared the corner across from the block Bree's house was on. As we hurried across the street, keeping to the alley-way, my heart pounded. When we approached her backyard, Bran effortlessly hopped the four-foot fence, landing behind an oak tree. The trunk was wide enough to offer cover for all three of us. Faron caught hold of my waist and boosted me up, and Bran helped me down to the other side. Faron joined us and we were in Bree's backyard. We kept to the shadow behind the tree, peeking out.

Faron held his finger to his lips, sniffing the air. Then, he leaned over to Bran and whispered something in his ear that I couldn't hear. Bran set off for the middle of the backyard. Taking me by the hand, Faron led me along the fence line to the edge of the yard. We turned and were soon in the shelter of the side yard, next to the fence dividing Bree's house from the graveyard.

We crept along, low to the ground. I was in decent shape, but my knees weren't used to squatting, and they didn't enjoy moving in this position. Faron had no trouble, but then again, he was used to shifting form and running.

I sighed. The truth was, I needed the gym I'd signed up for.

We reached the gate leading into the graveyard and Faron froze. He stared, squinting, and I tried to follow the direction he was looking in, but it was twilight now. While I could discern auras, I couldn't see in the dark. But the next moment he pointed and I leaned forward, trying to see what he was looking at. There, where the graveyard met the street, was the outline of a car parked along the curb. It could be a neighbor...or maybe someone else.

Faron leaned close and whispered, his breath tickling my ear. "That might be her stalker. He probably couldn't help himself and came back to the graveyard. Moth to flame."

"How do we find out?"

"There are places to hide in the cemetery. A couple of mausoleums, for one thing. Let's go." He cautiously rose, silently leaping the gate, then held out his hand as I climbed up on the middle slat of the gate, then swung my other leg over and jumped down.

We quickly slipped behind the yew that we had found the camera in. I scanned the graveyard. If the stalker was here, he could be hidden anywhere. I examined the tree where we'd found the camera and it didn't look like it had been replaced.

"Can you sense anybody?" Faron whispered.

I sat down against the tree, leaning my head back against the trunk, and closed my eyes.

I reached down and planted my hands against the ground, sending feelers through the soil, into the plants, using them as a conduit to discover any intruders. The plants picked up my query, and the question rippled along to the animals hiding among them.

Listening, I waited, as the energy rolled through the yard, touching each blade of grass, each leaf, every rabbit, vole, shrew, and mouse around. I could feel them stop quickly to examine the rolling wave, and carry on.

And then, an unexpected disturbance broke through the smoothly wending energy field—a disruption—as though an ocean wave had suddenly crashed around a rock.

I stiffened. Everything around the disturbance froze, on alert. There was a cat nearby, and she hissed and backed away. The grass bent under footsteps, and the light breeze that had sprung up billowed around the form.

A figure it was, but not a statue. No, the obstruction had an energy field of its own—*his* own, I ventured. The energy read masculine and dank. I tried to project my vision through the earth elemental who was helping me see, but everything was fuzzy when I tried to reduce it to a visual, and the attempt to do so broke the connection.

I stumbled back on my ass, sitting there, trying to figure out what had happened.

After a moment, I turned to Faron, who was watching me, confused as much as I was. I motioned for him to lean close. "There's someone out here with us, but before I could pinpoint where in the graveyard, it got disrupted. But it's a he, all right, and he spooks the locals, so to speak. The nature spirits and animals around the area."

"All right. Do you have any idea in which direction we should look?"

I glanced around, my gaze falling on one of the mausoleums. "There—I think that direction." It felt right. I gauged what we could still see of the graveyard. "We can get there if we sneak from yew tree to yew tree. The grass is high enough that, if we keep crouched down, there's a chance he won't see us."

"Sounds good to me. Let's go." Faron led the way, and we half crept, half crawled our way over to the next yew tree.

The trees were awake—they could sense our presence. Yew trees guarded the path between the world of the dead and the world of the living. Sentinels of the underworld, they were often found in old graveyards. The dark gods who walked in the shadows often carried staves made of yew, as did priestesses of the dead.

It took us ten minutes of cautious movement to near the mausoleum. From where we were hiding behind a sapling, we could see the door. It was ajar. Spirits wandered around the cemetery, and at that moment, a ghost exited the mausoleum and turned to look at me.

Dressed in what looked like a Victorian-style wedding dress, the ghost was more of a specter—with the flesh missing from her body. The skeleton carried a mist-shrouded bouquet and long blond hair still flowed from where it was attached to her skull. Fire burned in her eyes, and she seemed more vital and aware than most of the other spirits in this graveyard.

She fastened her gaze onto me, the twin flames in her sockets blazing like burning coal. She moved forward, and I quickly sensed an animosity toward me as she stopped in front of our hiding spot. I wanted to shout for her to go away, but that would give away our presence. I had no idea if the stalker could see ghosts—if he could, and he was near, he'd notice the kerfuffle. If he didn't, then he probably wouldn't notice us unless I was stupid and actually said something.

What do you want in my kingdom? the skeleton bride asked.

I glanced up at her, not wanting to speak. Time to find out if she could hear my thoughts. *We aren't here to disturb the dead—we mean you no harm. Our quarry is one of the living. We seek him alone. We do not aim to disrupt you or your subjects.* Until now, I mostly had spoken aloud to the dead, but it was time to see if I could reach them on their own level.

Apparently, it worked. She stared at me a moment longer, then said, *Then be about your business and leave my shadowy kingdom as soon as you can. Your quarry resides within the mausoleum walls. Take him and get him out of our way. The living aren't welcome here.*

I longed to tell her that we didn't want to be here, either, but decided to take my victories where I could. I quickly whispered what had happened to Faron.

He shivered. "There are ghosts walking around us right now?"

"Never mind the ghosts. Did you hear what I said? The guy's inside."

"Yes, I heard what you said. But I'm not too keen on ghosts." Faron frowned, then moved in front of me. "Let me go first."

My first instinct was to be annoyed, but then I checked myself. He was strong and he was skilled in fighting. I was neither. I followed him as he stood and darted across the five yards separating us from the mausoleum.

We reached the edge of the granite structure and pressed up against the wall. Faron slowly inched around the front, with me following him. Another step closer to the open door, then another. Faron held up his hand and, fingers counting down from three, he motioned for me to follow him. On the count of one, we slipped around the cracked door, pushing our way in. A moment later, I pulled out my flashlight and turned it on.

The light illuminated the inner sanctum, showing four sarcophagi, laid out in a diamond pattern. A small window high up on the back wall allowed a sliver of light to enter, but right now, all I could see was the glint of the glass.

I looked around, but I didn't see anybody. "I don't understand. I *know* I felt him in here." I spoke as softly as I could.

"Well, I don't see him now. Is there another way out?" Faron examined the walls as I followed him, holding the light as he tried to find any secret exits.

"Not that I can see," I said, squinting over his shoulder. "I still... He was in here. I could feel him. I could feel—"

But I didn't get a chance to finish my sentence, as something hard hit my head and everything went black.

CHAPTER FIFTEEN

THE FIRST THING I NOTICED WAS THAT MY HEAD HURT. Bad. The second thing I noticed was that I was cold and lying on something hard. Squinting, I slowly pushed my way up, sitting on what I now realized was a cold stone floor. I tried to look around but it was pitch dark, and I couldn't see anything.

Where was I? What had happened? And then, I remembered—I'd been with Faron. So, where was he? I'd also been holding a flashlight. I felt around me, trying to find something that would tell me if I was still in the mausoleum.

Something raced over my hand and I yanked my hand off the floor, trying not to shriek. I didn't want to alert anybody that I was here.

There are few venomous creatures over this side of the Cascades, I reminded myself. *There shouldn't be any black widows or scorpions or rattlesnakes.*

A moment later, I ran into something solid and cool—I felt along the sides and realized it was about four feet high. The material felt like stone, so I pulled myself up to my feet. I still felt woozy from the knot on my head. Holding onto the edge, I crept my way around the stone outcropping and quickly realized that it was a sarcophagus. Maybe I *was* still in the mausoleum.

I tried to remember the position of the sarcophagi—they had been arranged in a diamond, so I made my way to the end and staggered forward. Not ten steps later, I bumped into the end of another one. Since I'd been at the back of the mausoleum, I suspected that the exit would be on the other end of this stone coffin. I felt my way around it, holding onto it for both balance and direction. When I came to the end, I let go and kept walking forward, hands out.

I wavered, my head spinning with pain and wooziness, but a few steps later my hands ran into a wall. I felt around and found the door handle and, shoving with my shoulder, I opened the door and stumbled out into the dark of night.

I gasped as the chill air hit me. Nights were cool on the peninsula, even during summer. Shivering, I was grateful that I'd brought the jacket. But now that I knew where I was, what the hell had happened? And where was Faron?

As I waited for my eyes to adjust, I heard a dog bark and Oscar ran up to me, barking loudly. He bumped against me, whining. I petted his ears.

"Crap, if you're out—"

I'd no more started to speak when Atlas joined us. He was limping, from what I could see in the starlight that shone down on us. I felt for my phone, but couldn't find it. Double crap. It was probably on the floor in the mausoleum.

"Come on, boys, help me back to your house. I need to check on Bree and call the cops." I pressed my hands against them and felt them respond. I leaned down, focusing on what I needed to accomplish, and they seemed to pick up on it. They stayed by my side and, with me stumbling along, guided me to the gate dividing the cemetery from Bree's house.

We reached the porch a few minutes later. Thank gods,

the light was on and I was able to see that the door had been busted open. I quickly turned to the dogs and saw that Atlas had blood on his hindquarters. I hustled them inside and immediately I could see that a struggle had taken place.

My knees buckling, I dropped into a chair. I needed my phone. Bree didn't have a landline, and the gods only knew where her phone was. I tried to sort out what to do, but I couldn't think clearly. My head was still foggy from the blow I'd taken. It was at that moment that I remembered Bran had been in the side yard. Was he still there? If so, why hadn't he noticed the dogs out?

But then, I sensed something—the smallest glimmer of a *Hello?*

"Who's that? Who's trying to contact me?" It was easier to ask the question aloud, given how my thoughts were drifting.

Elphyra, are you all right? The voice was familiar, and I caught a glimpse of Fancypants. Of course—*we were bonded*! I still didn't know what that all entailed, but obviously, it included a rudimentary mind-link.

"Thank gods! Fancypants, I'm at Bree's. I need help. Tell Grams to call Daisy and the medics! Hurry!"

Will do. Be safe.

I tried to stand, to head toward the kitchen, when Bran staggered through the kitchen door. He was bleeding from a gash on his forehead, but he was on his feet.

"Elphyra, are you okay?"

I started to shake my head but it hurt too much. "No, I think I have a concussion. I can't find Bree or Faron."

He pulled out his phone. "I'll call the sheriff."

"You still have your phone? Thank the gods." I dropped back on the sofa. I desperately wanted to go look for Bree and Faron, but I was too shaky. Getting into the house had taken everything I had left.

Bran called Daisy, only to find that Grams had called her minutes before. Daisy said she'd called an ambulance.

"She's on her way," Bran added as he hung up. "Daisy, that is. It took her quite the argument but she convinced your great-grandmother to stay home. My mother's going up to stay with her."

I was slipping in and out of consciousness. Bran tried to wake me up, but I was having more and more trouble keeping focused. By the time the medics arrived, I was mostly out of it, though I was able to answer some basic questions. Another crew was taking care of Bran.

Daisy entered the living room and I managed to give her a semi-lucid story.

"So, you didn't see what happened to Faron?"

"Whoever it was probably hit me first. Have you been out to check the mausoleum yet?"

"I sent Arnie and a couple of the men out—" she stopped as the door open and Arnie rushed in.

"We found Faron. The medics are with him now." He glanced at me, his face grim. He handed me a phone. "Is this yours?"

I took it, sitting forward as I tried to focus. "Yeah. Is he okay? Is Faron okay?"

Arnie glanced over at Bran, and the look between them chilled me to the bone. Bran shrugged off the medics and moved over next to me. He wrapped his arm around me as I waited, my heart racing.

"We don't know. He's alive, but he's unresponsive. He was hit over the head as well, but it looks like the blow was worse than yours. He's on his way to the hospital now." Arnie ducked his head. "I'm sorry."

I shook my head. Everything felt like it was swirling. My fiancé had been dragged away from me in a violent attack. Now, Faron was headed to the hospital, unconscious. Was it me? Had I jinxed him by sleeping with him? I burst into tears, both confused from the concussion and terrified for Faron.

"Faron's in the hospital, Bree's missing. What the hell are we going to do?" I turned to Daisy. "Do you know anything about Bree?"

"Actually, we have a break. We already have a match on the fingerprints we found in the mausoleum, and in the house —they were on a knife we found on the kitchen floor, and on the door." Daisy consulted her notes. "Does the name 'Evan Taylor' ring a bell?"

I frowned, trying to concentrate. Somewhere, in the back of my mind, the name rang an alarm, but I couldn't place it. I shook my head. "It sounds familiar, but I can't remember where I heard it."

"How about Fort Worden High School? Does that help?"

That was a blast from the past. I leaned my head back, trying to keep awake.

Evan Taylor. Evan Taylor...back from my high school days.

As I tried to think, a face rippled into view, a face from high school.

A tall, lean boy, leaning against the wall while holding his books, waiting for Bree and me as we walked down the hallway. As we passed him, he stepped out in front of us. I stopped, staring at him. I didn't like Evan. He was creepy, and he was always watching Bree. Bree ignored him for the most part, but this day, she couldn't.

"Go to the dance with me," he said, his gaze darting to the side.

Bree let out a sigh. "Get out of the way, Evan. I'm not going to the dance with you."

Evan narrowed his eyes. "I said, go to the dance with me."

"Forget it. I already have a date. And if you want to ask me, ask nicely—you don't tell a girl she has to go out with you. That's... creepy AF."

"Seriously," I said. "That's fucked up. Leave us alone."

Evan glared at me, and his look unsettled me. I looked away, not wanting to get involved. His mouth twisted in an unpleasant fashion and he slunk away, vanishing into the lunch crowd. Bree and I shrugged, and continued on with our day...

"Oh crap. Evan Taylor was *always* hovering around her, all through middle school and part of high school. Then he disappeared." I struggled to sit up straight. "Do you know where he is? Does he still live in Port Townsend?"

"No, he moved to Starlight Hollow a few years ago. I'm headed over to his house now."

"We need to get Elphyra to the hospital—" Bran started to say, but I interrupted.

"No. I want to go with you." I tried to stand up and once again, a wave of dizziness swept over me.

"You can't. You'll slow them down," Bran said. "I'll go with them. You go to the hospital." He motioned to the medics. "She should be in the hospital, shouldn't she?"

"That's what we'd recommend, sir." One of the medics came over and led me to a chair. "You really need medical treatment. Let us take you in now, or we'll require you to sign a waiver verifying you've refused treatment."

I stopped fighting. In my heart, I knew that I couldn't help Bree in the shape I was in. I looked over at Bran. "Find her, please. Find her and save her."

Daisy, Arnie, and Bran headed out the door, leaving me sitting there with the medics. Atlas and Oscar whined, huddling near the rocking chair. I couldn't leave them there, and I couldn't take them to the hospital. I called Doctor John's emergency number and explained the situation. "I'm sorry, but I couldn't think of anybody else to call."

"Can you drop them off at the office? I can be there in ten minutes."

I thanked him and asked one of the deputies still at the house if they could drive Oscar and Atlas over to the vet's office. He agreed, passing them off to his partner. I gave them the address and then let the medics move me to a stretcher. I wanted to stay, to be here when they brought Bree home. I couldn't let myself think that she might not be okay. I couldn't go there.

I leaned back on the stretcher and closed my eyes, surrendering to the gentle movement of the stretcher. Before we made it to the ambulance, I passed into unconsciousness.

THE SOUNDS in the background registered through the fog. Something was beeping nearby, and there was some sort of rhythmic swooping. In the distance, several bells rang, and the muffled sound of voices filled every direction. It felt like I was being held down, but it didn't feel like I was being restrained. I was lying in a bed, it seemed, but on an incline— my back was propped up.

Taking a deep breath, I opened my eyes and confirmed what I thought. I was in a hospital room, with an IV in my arm, and several gadgets hooked up to me. To my right, a nurse was monitoring a machine. To my left, Grams sat by my bed.

"Grams?" I struggled to sit up but the nurse immediately turned and gently pushed me back.

"Elphyra! You're awake!" Grams seldom expressed excitement but now, she jumped up and moved over to take my hand.

"How long have I been out? Did they find Bree?"

"Not yet, love, but Bran's still out there with Sheriff Parker. It's nearly four A.M. You were brought in about ninety minutes ago." Grams tugged my sheet up and tucked it in around me. "How are you feeling?"

I gauged my body. "My head hurts. I ache all over, but I

STARLIGHT DREAMS

think that's more exhaustion than anything. Did I say my
head hurts?" I tried to remember everything that had gone
on. Bree was still missing. Bran was out searching for her.
And... "Faron. How's Faron? Is he here, in the hospital too?"

Grams glanced over at the doctor and stepped away from
the bed. The doctor took her place.

"There's no easy way to say this, so I'll be direct. Your
friend Faron is in critical condition. We're going to have to
place him in a medically induced coma, in hopes of relieving
some of the pressure on his brain."

The words registered, but it was too much to handle. I
leaned back against the bed again, closing my eyes. "This
can't be happening. This can't be real."

"Unfortunately, it's all too real. We've contacted his next
of kin. I think he's in the waiting room, if you'd like to talk to
him. His brother, Kyle."

"Please ask if he's willing to come in. How long do I have
to stay here?" Everything was a mess. Bree was still missing,
Faron was critically injured, and Bran was hurt. "Nothing's
going right," I added, turning to Grams.

"Hold strong, my dear. When things are bad, you must
hold on to that inner core of strength." Grams gazed at me,
and I could feel her pain below the surface. She was as
worried as I was, but she was holding it together so I could
lean on her.

"I so wish I could be like you," I said. "Strong enough to
face bad news without breaking down."

"Sometimes you need a shoulder, my dear. And I am your
shoulder. You're exhausted, in pain, and suffering the afteref-
fects of a bad concussion. But fate doesn't play favorites, and
she doesn't excuse anyone from her blows, or her wins."
Grams held out her hand again and I took it, squeezing
tightly.

"I'll have one of the aides talk to Kyle Collinsworth," the

171

doctor said. "We're inducing the coma now—and to ease your mind, several doctors, including me, concurred that this is Faron's best chance of survival."

"All right. How long am I in here for?"

"We want to hold you for a few hours to make certain the concussion isn't worse than we think before we send you home. You'll need to rest up for a few days, but you should be all right." The doctor turned to the nurse. "I'll check back on six-o'clock rounds."

As he left, the aide returned with Kyle. The wolf shifter looked uncomfortable and somber, but that was understandable, given the circumstances. I motioned him over to the bed.

"Kyle, right? You took care of the wasps' nest for me."

"Yes, Ms. MacPherson. I'm so sorry this happened—"

"Call me Elphyra. I'm sorry Faron got caught in the middle." I tried to hold the tears back, but one slipped out and down my cheek. "I wish we'd waited for backup. Our plan went horribly wrong."

"How are you feeling?" Kyle had the same caring look as his brother, though it felt less personal and more polite.

"Rough. Our friend Bran was hurt, too." I wasn't sure what to say now that Kyle was here. "What will happen till Faron's brought out of the coma?"

"I'll be acting King. Then we'll wait and see. If he isn't healed up in six months, I'll be installed as the actual King. Can you tell me more about what happened? They're not equipped with anything but the medical side here."

"Sit down," Grams said, standing and offering her chair. "I think I'll go get myself some coffee." She headed out of the room before I could protest.

Kyle drew the chair closer and sat down. "Please tell me what was going on."

I told him the whole story—how Faron was helping Bree,

that we were after a stalker who had still managed to kidnap her, that I was worried sick about my best friend.

"I'll do what I can to help," Kyle said. "I don't want Faron's sacrifice to go in vain, and in our commune, we don't allow mistreatment of women or children." He paused, then said, "Are you my brother's girlfriend?"

I hesitated. "I don't know how to answer that. Faron and I are involved, but...I don't know *what* we are yet. We started out as adversaries, but...sometimes a spark turns into a blaze and becomes passion instead of ire." I blushed. "Maybe that's TMI but..."

"No, it gives me an idea of what you mean to him. And what he means to you. I'm sorry, you must be worried sick." Kyle, the bee man, reached out to take my hand. "Don't worry, he'll be all right. He *has* to be okay."

"I hope so," I said. "I can't take another loss like..." I met his gaze as he waited. "I lost my fiancé last year. I can't take another heartbreak."

And all Kyle could do was nod.

CHAPTER SIXTEEN

IT WAS EARLY MORNING AND GRAMS AND I WERE SITTING in the back of the Town Car and driver she kept on retainer. We were on the way home. There was no word from Bran yet, no word from Daisy, and now Faron rested in the depths of his subconscious, unaware of time passing by around him.

Grams said nothing, just held my hand as the car passed through the glimmering rays of dawn. The sun was waking up, the world was beginning its routine again, and I felt totally out of sync with everything around me.

We arrived home and Grams helped me into the house. She shut the door behind us and deposited me on the sofa. Fancypants had curled up to sleep on the rocking chair and he woke, flying over to sit on the back of the sofa.

"May's asleep in the guest room," he said. "She spent a long time playing with the kittens. You look like you've been through a couple rounds in the ring."

"I feel like it," I said. I was still exhausted, but the hydration and pain meds had gone a long way to making me feel better. I took a deep breath and let it out slowly. "But I want real food, not hospital fare. Leftovers would be fine, if we have any," I added.

Grams vanished into the kitchen without a word. Fancy-pants snuggled in by my side. "Tell me what happened."

Once again, I repeated the events of the night. By the time I finished, Grams was back with a mug of chicken noodle soup and a couple slices of toast. After I ate, I realized I was slipping back on the cushions, and once again, I was out like a light.

BY TEN A.M., I was sitting at the table. The knot on my head still hurt, but otherwise, I felt like I'd pulled a drunken bender that ended in a massive hangover. Grams was taking a nap and May was keeping a watch on me.

"You can go home, really." I stared at my latte that May had grudgingly made me. She'd wanted to make me tea but I wasn't interested.

"Your great-grandmother would have my hide. She needs her sleep." May stared out of the kitchen window. "I wish they'd call."

"I'd call Daisy, but I don't want to chance interrupting anything important. But maybe a text..." Texts could interrupt matters, too, but at least they were less intrusive. I pulled out my phone and texted both Daisy and Bran.

IS EVERYTHING OKAY? WE'VE BEEN WAITING TO HEAR FROM YOU FOR HOURS.

I waited, but there was no answer. "Do you have Find a Friend on your phone, for Bran?"

"No, unfortunately I don't. That's going to change." As she opened her phone, the doorbell rang.

"I'll get it—and yes, I'm quite capable of opening the

door." I headed to the door, followed by Fancypants. He hovered around me, more concerned than my Grams.

I opened the door and saw Arnie. His face was ashen and he looked shaken. "Have you heard from Bran or Daisy?" he asked.

My heart sank. "I just texted them, but no—I don't think so. Let me look to make sure they didn't text me while I was in the hospital." Although I knew they hadn't, a part of me really wanted to be wrong. I looked but no texts had come through from Bree since before Faron and I'd been attacked. And at three A.M., Bran had left one text that he was still out with Daisy.

I showed Arnie. "What do you think has happened to them?" I asked as I invited him in.

"We're not sure. We arrived at Evan Taylor's house at about two-thirty. There was no one there, but we had probable cause to search his place. We found a room filled with pictures of Bree, so we know he's most likely the stalker, but we couldn't find any sign of her."

"Where does he live? Tell me, because you know I can find out."

Arnie gave me Evan's address. "I don't know what to do. We're going to call in the FBI if we haven't found them by this evening." He paused. "How are you doing?"

"Sore. One hell of a headache." I told him about Faron. "I'm so worried."

"That's scary," Arnie said. He paused, then asked, "Are you and Faron…"

"An item? Kind of. We're headed that way," I said. "What should I tell May about—"

"About what?" May joined us. She looked from Arnie's face to mine. "You haven't heard from them?"

He shook his head. "The sheriff sent me back to the station after Evan's house was a bust."

But something rang off about what he was saying—not that he was lying, but there was something that had gotten overlooked. Something they hadn't seen. My instincts were yelling at me now.

"Did you examine his house thoroughly?"

"Yes, we did. We found nothing. His car wasn't there, either, and we have an APB out on him. We also have an APB out on Sheriff Parker's car." Arnie stood up. "Well, if you hear from either of them, let us know."

I saw him out, then returned to the sofa, where I curled up beneath a throw and focused on Bree, Daisy, and Bran. *Boom,* images of a dark space, slightly damp but warm, flashed into my mind. I focused on the walls, trying to see what they were like, and reached out my hand. Another *boom*, and I felt damp wood beneath my fingers. I could smell the tang of soil, that pungent smell of damp earth. Petrichor.

"Elphyra, are you okay?" May's voice penetrated the fog.

"Yeah, but I'm getting something. Can you lead me as I describe what I'm seeing?" I still wasn't focused enough to guide myself.

May settled in next to me and took my right hand. I held out my left hand and closed my eyes again. "I'm in a dark space—with wooden walls to the left and right. There's a feeling of dampness in the air, I can smell soil, like freshly turned. It smells like it's been raining."

"Do you see anything else around? Is there any illumination?" May's voice was calm and collected and she made me feel safe.

I looked around. There was a faint glow from behind me, and I turned, trying to discern where it was coming from. There—at the end of the passage I was in, the light was coming from there. I followed it, my footsteps making a ghostly sound.

"My steps—it sounds like I'm walking on concrete. I'm at

the end of the tunnel. To my right, I see a room—there's a door and the light is coming from behind the door."

May paused, then asked, "Walk back the other way. What do you see? How long is the corridor?"

I turned and headed back the other way. "It's long...like a long hallway. The light's fading behind me but I can still see. *Why* can I see?" I glanced up and saw that I was nearing a staircase at the end of the hall, ascending to the left. Above the bottom step, at least ten feet up, was a window. It was grimy—with lots of dirt, but there was light coming from outside. "I see a window. I think I'm in a basement."

"Go up the stairs, please." May was good in guiding the journey.

I ascended the stairs, pausing on the fourth. "There are two broken stairs, fourth and fifth from the bottom. I'm stepping over them." In my astral form, I didn't hurt, although the headache interfered with my ability to focus. "I'm nearly at the top now," I said after skipping the steps and continuing up. At the top, I stopped. There was a door, but when I stepped through it, I found myself in a kitchen. I turned back to see a bookcase against the wall that I'd walked through.

"There's a bookcase on the other side of the door. I walked through the bookcase and now I'm in the kitchen." I looked around. There was a light on over the stove. Was this Evan's house? But the cops had been here. Yet...I looked back at the bookshelf. Had the cops thought to look behind it? But why should they? It looked like any normal bookcase, filled with books. They wouldn't have thought to see if there was a door behind it. I returned to the wall and once again, crossed through the bookcase, and went back down into the secret basement.

"I'm heading to the end of the hall again."

"Do you hear anything? Smell anything?"

I listened. "I hear... I think I hear someone talking. As far as smell, the mildew smell is strong. I'm following the hallway to the end and going through that door."

Heading down the hall, I went through the door. As I entered the room, I gasped. There, against the back of the room, was a cell, like a jail cell. And behind the bars, I saw Bran, sprawled on the floor, and Daisy, who was chained to the wall as she sat on a stark iron bunk. Her head was down, and she looked as out of it as Bran did.

I glanced at a small table and chair outside the cell and on it, I saw a bottle of pills that had been spilled on the table. Bran suddenly sat up—or at least, his spirit did. He was still connected to his body. I could see the silver cord binding him. He looked at me and—as clear as day—I heard him say, "Help us, Elphyra. Please, help us."

Immediately, I shook myself out of the trance, snapping back in my body so hard and fast that I made myself dizzy. "I have to go. I found Bran and Daisy—and I need to get to them now. Where are my keys?"

"You can't drive in your condition," May said.

"Then you'll have to drive me. Come on, we have no time to waste." I turned to Fancypants. "Tell Grams we've gone to save Daisy and Bran. I'll call Arnie on the way."

Fancypants didn't try to stop me. "Go. I will tell Grams. Be safe."

I felt an intense wave of caring and love coming from him. "Be good with the kittens. Damn, I didn't feed them—"

"I did," May said. "Come on. They'll be fine till we get back."

I hustled out the door behind her, keeping my balance with Gram's walking stick, which I'd grabbed from near the coatrack. May's car was in the driveway and at that point, I realized that the shop was still going to be closed. Well, it was too late. I also glanced at my phone and saw a reminder for the gym this morning. Had it been only two days since I'd bought my membership? Well, another strike against my schedule.

I turned back to Fancypants before closing the door. "Ask Grams to put up an emergency note on the store that I'm closed today, please." And then, I followed May down to her car, where I climbed in and, phone at my ear, I called Arnie.

WE REACHED Evan Taylor's house before Arnie and, though he'd told me to wait for him, I jumped out and hurried up the steps. Evan was gone, and so Bree was nowhere to be found, but Daisy and Bran were here and they were in danger. I tried the door, but it was locked. Then I remembered the window that overlook the basement. I circled the house, finally discovering the window behind a thicket of ivy and jasmine. I stripped away the vines, feeling bad for destroying them, but I'd apologize later. After a few moments, the window was accessible. It was so well hidden that I wasn't surprised that the cops had missed it.

May caught up to me and pulled a pair of shears out of her apron. She cut back the bigger vines as I dragged them out. I was running on pure adrenaline. The sense of urgency had grown so great that I was frantic, and I struggled so hard that I landed on my ass, a huge clump of ivy in my arms.

"Are you all right?" May asked, hurrying over to my side.

I stood. "Yeah, I am. Look—I can get through to break the window now. Hand me... There's a brick over there. Will you grab it for me?"

May bent and hefted the large brick, which she cautiously gave to me. "Be careful, it's heavy."

I took the brick and turned back to the window. "Here

goes nothing," I muttered, heaving the brick toward the glass. It shattered the pane on contact, and I moved in. There were shards of glass everywhere, and I turned back to May. "Give me your apron?"

She didn't ask why, just untied it and handed it to me, taking her keys out of the pocket along with her wallet.

I wrapped the apron around my hand and used it to wipe away the slivers of glass around the frame. "I'm going in. Stay here and watch for the police. I hope they called an ambulance."

Kneeling at the edge of the window, I looked down into the gloom. There was the bottom of the staircase, like I'd seen in my vision. Gingerly, I sat on the edge, praying there weren't enough slivers of glass left to pierce my butt, and then —taking a deep breath—I pushed off, dropping to the floor, where I fell forward into the shattered glass. Gently, I used the wall to help me stand up. My head was killing me, my hands were bleeding from a few shards of glass that had lodged in my palms, and my vision blurred for a moment before clearing enough for me to head down the hallway.

I came to the door at the end and tried the knob. It turned without resistance and I shoved it open. Like I had seen in my astral journey, there was a cell against the back wall, and inside, I saw Bran and Daisy. I raced over, but the cell door was locked.

"Damn it! Where are you, Arnie? Hurry up!" I clanged on the bars. "Daisy! Bran! Wake up! Can you hear me?"

Neither responded. I squinted in the dim light coming from the bare bulb on the ceiling. I could see the faint movements of their chests, but the sound of their breathing was labored. Grabbing out my phone, I called Arnie again.

"I'm almost there—"

"Daisy and Bran are here. I found them. They're drugged,

I think. Are the medics on the way? I can't get to them because they're locked in a cell."

"I have bolt cutters in the trunk, along with a toolbox. I'll bring it when I—I'm pulling into the driveway. I'll see you in a few minutes. Can you find out what drug they've been given?"

"Maybe. Hurry." I crossed to the table and looked at the tablets. They were narrow, bar-like, and white. There were maybe twenty of them scattered on the table. I glanced at the prescription bottle. The name had been blacked out by a black pen, but the bottle listed the number prescribed as fifty. Had Bran and Daisy been forced to take thirty between them?

"Crap! That's too many." Bran and Daisy were dying and there was nothing I could do. If I worked with air magic, I might be able to force oxygen into their lungs. But—

I could hear the door to the basement open and footsteps leading down. "Elphyra?" Arnie appeared. He took one look at the cell and at Daisy's and Bran's silent figures and raced over, his bolt cutters in one hand, his toolbox in the other.

"They've been drugged. They're dying. Hurry!" I followed him, wanting to help.

He looked around. "No keys?"

I shook my head. "Not that I found."

"Stand back," he said, handing me the tools and the bolt cutters. He brought out his gun and, aiming carefully, added, "Move back and cover your ears."

I dropped the tools and hurried back to the door, where I covered my ears. "Go!"

Arnie pulled the trigger and shot the lock. The reverbera-tion hurt my ears as the smell of gunpowder filled the air, but the cell door clicked and swung open. As he pushed it wide, I could hear the medics enter the house and come dashing down the stairs.

Arnie moved back as I showed them the pills. The paramedics glanced at the bottle, then at the pills, then they moved in to help Bran and Daisy. By then, May had found her way down to me, and I put my arm around her as she stiffened, staring at the scene.

"He'll be okay. I think we found them in time." I prayed that was the case, but I had no idea. I could only hold my breath and hope.

"Please, let him—" May stopped as one of the paramedics came over.

"You found them in time," the paramedic confirmed. "They'll need a couple days in the hospital, their stomachs pumped, but they'll survive. We're getting them stabilized for the trip to the hospital now."

I let out a long breath as May slumped against me, tearing up.

"Oh, thank the gods," she whispered. "My son..."

"You can meet us at the hospital." The medic moved off, and I turned, arm around May's shoulder, and walked her out of the way.

"Come on. Let's go—"

Arnie came rushing up. "We're following Bran's truck. It was missing, as well, so we put out an APB on it too."

I stiffened. "Is it Evan? Does he have Bree?"

"We're not sure—our deputies are in pursuit right now." He glanced at May. "Why don't you head to the hospital and I'll let you know the moment we find out if Bree's in the truck."

As much as I wanted to stay and find out, I followed May out. We exited up the stairs, through the bookcase door, and headed for May's car.

"Are you good to drive?" I asked.

She nodded. "I'm fine. Bran's going to survive. I can manage driving us to the hospital." She waited till I buckled my seat belt and we headed out. I glanced back at the house, and I knew why I'd been able to find them. I had connected to Bran. I hadn't realized it before, but I had connected to that massively warm heart of his and the magical blood we both had, had linked. So I was able to pinpoint where they were being held. And I held onto that thought, all the way to the hospital.

CHAPTER SEVENTEEN

MAY AND I WERE SITTING IN THE WAITING ROOM AS ARNIE called.

"We caught him. And he had Bree in the truck with him —she's alive. She's on her way to the hospital, too." He paused and I could hear a "but" behind the hesitation.

"How is she?" I asked, not wanting to hear what I was afraid I was going to hear.

"She's pretty bruised up. I can't tell you the extent, because that's confidential, but Elphyra, she's going to need some help recovering from this. You have the background to empathize." By the tone of his voice, it wasn't good.

"What about Evan?"

"He's in custody. We'll make sure he never touches her again. We were careful to take our time and do everything right so when he goes to court, he can't claim any technicalities."

I gulped a shallow breath and tried to restrain my anger. I wanted to kill him—to tear him apart. "Thanks, Arnie. You sure you can't find a ravine to dump..."

I stopped. I didn't want to say the wrong thing, to add

anything to the chance he might go free. But if I could work death magic, Evan Taylor would be six feet under, never to walk the world again. I'd seen too much death, too much torture, too much evil. I wanted vengeance. I wanted justice.

"I know what you were going to say," Arnie said. "Trust me, if I could oblige, I would. But you and I know that's not acceptable in society."

"I know," I whispered. "If Faron...dies...then Evan has a murder charge on his hands, as well as attempted murder, kidnapping, stalking, and who knows what else."

"Let's hope it doesn't come to that," he said.

At that moment, the doctor walked into the waiting room.

"I have to go. The doctor's here. I'll have him call you about Daisy."

"Thanks, Elphyra. You're one of the good ones, you know?" Arnie hung up.

The doctor had good news. Bran and Daisy were both on the mend. We had gotten to them in time. Daisy was still unconscious, but Bran was awake. May encouraged me to go back with her, though I first declined, wanting to give her time with her son.

Bran was lying there, hooked up to the same sort of machines that had been attached to me the night before. His gown was open, his chest showing, and his hair was still pulled back in a manbun.

"Hey," he said, his voice weak. He looked groggy, but the three IVs attached to him seemed to be making a difference.

May took his hand, kissing it as she leaned over him. "My dear, thank the gods you're alive and awake. You have Elphyra to thank for that."

I couldn't exactly brush off the accolade because I had been the one to find them, but I didn't want the spotlight. "Part of the kudos goes to your son, May. If Bran hadn't reached out and contacted me...I think that's why I ended up in the basement on the astral plane. He managed to touch my soul."

His eyes were shining as he stared up at me from the bed. "Thank you—you saved us. Is Bree—"

"They found her, along with Evan. They're bringing her into the hospital now," I said.

He reached for my hand, holding onto May's with the other. I wrapped my fingers around his hand and a spark raced up my arm, a spark of recognition and understanding. The look in his eyes told me he felt the connection too.

I caught my breath, then let it out slowly. "Bran...thank you for helping. I'm so glad you're all right."

"How are you?" he asked, his fingers caressing mine.

"Don't ask...not right now." I closed my eyes, enjoying the comfort I felt coming from him. I needed comfort. I needed a shoulder to rest my head against right now. Part of me wanted to climb in the bed with him, snuggle in his arms, and cry for as long as the tears flowed.

"I'll be back," I said, squeezing his hand. "I'm going to check on Faron."

As I left the room, I heard Bran asking May about him.

FARON WAS IN A QUIET, dark private room. He was attached to an array of machines—a ventilator, several IVs, a couple scanners, probably to monitor his heart, blood pressure, and brain functions. He looked so regal and yet, he felt so distant, a long ways away, out of touch.

His brother Kyle was sitting there, to one side. He nodded as I approached the bed. I held onto the rails, unsure whether I should say anything or not, so I turned to Kyle, looking for some sort of answer.

"Follow me," Kyle said, leading me out of the room. We sat in some chairs outside.

"I wanted to say something to him, but given they're trying to minimize his neural activity, I doubt if I should." I rubbed my head. The headache was getting worse again and I wanted to go home and rest. But I wasn't leaving till they brought Bree in.

"They've asked me to keep quiet around him. The room is soundproofed, though the alarms ring through. He's still not out of the woods, Elphyra. He could die. Or live. If he lives, there's a chance he won't wake up, or that he'll have brain damage when he does wake." Kyle leaned forward, a broken look on his face. "I love my brother. I don't want to be King. I don't want his spot. I want him to recover and..." He was wringing his hands and I reached out, taking one of them. I held it tight, letting him brace himself on me.

"I hesitate to ask, but what about your parents? Do you have any other siblings?"

"Our father was King, but he died from a heart attack. Our mother died of grief. It's possible, you know—someone can die from heartbreak." He leaned his elbows on his knees and pulled his hand back. "Faron dated a lot of women after his wife died...but he never talked about introducing any of them to me until he started talking about you."

I hung my head, letting the tears come. "I'm afraid for him. I don't know what to do—I want to help but I can't do a thing."

"You can hope. Right now, that's all any of us can do," he said. "Thank you, for crying for him. I can't cry. In our Pack, the women cry for us. We're a warrior race living in a time when we're outdated. But we keep to our traditions." Kyle straightened up. "Will you cry for him, for me?"

I gave him a gentle nod. It wasn't the time to talk about men and women and gender roles. His brother needed me to help him through this. It was the one thing I could do for Faron and for Kyle.

"I promise, I'll cry for him. And I'll keep hope."

"I'd better get back." He stood, letting out a long sigh.

"Do you mind if I come visit?" I asked.

"Please do. I'll be here twice a week, on Tuesdays and Thursdays at four, if you ever want to talk. And…thank you. I think my brother was…is? Falling in love with you." And with that, he went back in the room, leaving me out in the hall.

THE DOCTOR WOULDN'T LET me in to see Bree—not until they'd fully examined her. "I suggest you go home and rest. I'll have her call you," Dr. Marston said. She shook her head. "Don't be upset if she needs some time to process everything that's gone on before she talks to anybody. She's been through a lot, that I can tell you."

I called Grams, who sent a hired car to get me. As I entered the house, she was waiting for me, with pizza, cola, and ice cream.

"How's your head?"

"Screaming. But…we saved Bran and Daisy, and Bree. Evan Taylor left a trail of damage in his wake, though." I glanced at Grams. "Do you know any spells to target someone from a distance?"

Grams motioned for me to follow her. I walked into the kitchen and found the kittens playing in a soft-sided pen next to the table. Immediately, I dropped to my knees and lifted first Gem, then Silver, out of the pen and hugged them.

"I needed this," I said, noticing that Fancypants was also in the pen. "Hey, what are you doing?"

"Getting to know them. I love them already," he said, his eyes alight.

"I'm glad. I thought you might have fun with them." I sighed, kissing Gem on the nose. "I'm sorry, little one. I haven't had much time since I brought you home yesterday."

"What did you mean about targeting someone?" Grams asked, setting the table. "Come, eat."

I put the kittens back in the pen and, after Fancypants flew up and over to his chair, I zipped the cover to the pen closed. The kittens could see us through the mesh sides but couldn't get out. Sitting at the table, I let Grams serve me. She handed me a super-strength headache powder and I poured it in my soda, stirring it and drinking it down.

"What I meant...Evan's hurt so many people, and if Faron dies, that will go up to murder. I'm not sure of everything he did to Bree in the time he had her, but apparently it wasn't good. I can't talk to her until she decides to call me. The doctor warned me about pushing her. Evan hurt Bran, he hurt me...and you know how justice works."

Grams considered the question. "Well, what we *can* do is a spell asking that justice be met full force. That he be visited by everything that he's done to others. Any darker spells, I will not teach you."

"If that's as strong as we can go, I want to go there."

As we ate, I decompressed. It hit me that I wasn't crying. I wasn't feeling weak, though I felt like I'd been hit by a truck. I was changing, and I had Grams to thank for that. She was having an effect on me, and it was a good one.

I stared at the cats, then at Fancypants and Grams. My life had joy in it now. As my thoughts turned to Faron, I quickly pulled them away. Right now, I couldn't handle one more painful moment. I needed to breathe. I needed to let go of all the darkness that had surrounded me in the past year.

But somewhere, in the depths of my mind, I heard the sound of bells. They were chiming, warning me that there were still challenges to come. Images of Bran and Faron flashed through my mind. The three of us weren't done. And Bree—she would need me to be strong as well. As to where we were all going, I had no clue, but the future was on the move and nothing would hold it back.

"What are you thinking?" Grams asked.

I shrugged. "I don't know," I said, not wanting to burden her with all of my dark thoughts. Instead, I turned the conversation to the cats, and Fancypants chimed in, and we ate dinner as the summer sun faded into twilight, and my future drew another step closer with every passing moment.

FOR MORE OF the Starlight Hollow Series, you can preorder Elphyra's third book. Together with her red drag-onette—Fancypants—she both protects *and* heats up the town in every sense of the word. Preorder the third book, **Starlight Demons**, now!

For more of the Moonshadow Bay Series:: January Jaxson returns to the quirky town of Moonshadow Bay after her husband dumps her and steals their business, and within days she's working for Conjure Ink, a paranormal investigations agency, and exploring the potential of her hot new neighbor. Ten books are currently available. You can preorder **Dreamer's Web** and **Woodland Web** now! If you haven't read the other books in this series, begin with **Starlight Web**.

For all the rest of my current and finished series, check out my State of the Series page, and you can also check the Bibliography at the end of this book, or check out my website at **Galenorn.com** and be sure and sign up for my **newsletter** to receive news about all my new releases. Also, you're welcome to join my YouTube Channel community.

QUALITY CONTROL: This work has been professionally edited and proofread. If you encounter any typos or formatting issues ONLY, please contact me through my **website** so they may be corrected. Otherwise, know that this book is in my style and voice and editorial suggestions will not be entertained. Thank you.

PLAYLIST

I often write to music, and STARLIGHT DREAMS was no exception. Here's the playlist I used for this book. You'll notice a distinct difference from most of my playlists, but this is what the mood of the book wanted.

- **Alice in Chains:** Man in the Box
- **Android Lust:** Here and Now
- **The Animals:** Story of Bo Diddley; Bury My Body
- **The Asteroids Galaxy Tour:** The Sun Ain't Shining No More; Heart Attack; The Golden Age; Around the Bend; Major
- **Awolnation:** Sail
- **Beats Antique:** Runaway; Vardo; Tabla Toy
- **Beck:** Emergency Exit; Farewell Ride
- **The Bravery:** Believe
- **Brent Lewis:** Beyond Midnight; Joy
- **Broken Bells:** The Ghost Inside
- **Celtic Woman:** The Butterfly
- **Chris Isaak:** Wicked Game

- **Circle of Women:** Mother of Darkness
- **Clannad:** Banba Óir; I See Red
- **Cream:** Strange Brew
- **Creedence Clearwater Revival:** Born on the Bayou
- **Crosby, Stills, & Nash:** Guinnevere
- **David Bowie:** Without You; China Girl
- **David & Steve Gordon:** Shaman's Drum Dance; Eagle's Rhythm Gift
- **Dead Can Dance:** Yulunga; The Ubiquitous Mr. Lovegrove; Indus
- **Deuter:** Petite Fleur
- **Dizzi:** Dizzi Jig; Dance of the Unicorns
- **DJ Shah:** Mellomaniac
- **Donovan:** Sunshine Superman; Season of the Witch
- **Dragon Ritual Drummers:** Black Queen; The Fall
- **Eastern Sun:** Beautiful Being
- **Enya:** Orinoco Flow
- **Everlast:** Ends; Black Jesus
- **Faun:** Rad; Sieben
- **Finger Eleven:** Paralyzer
- **Fleetwood Mac:** The Chain
- **Flight of the Hawk:** Bones
- **Foster the People:** Pumped Up Kicks
- **Gabrielle Roth:** The Calling; Raven; Cloud Mountain; Rest Your Tears Here; Zone Unknown; Avenue A
- **Godsmack:** Voodoo
- **Gorillaz:** Rockit; Stylo; Hongkongaton; Clint Eastwood; Dare; Demon Days
- **Halsey:** Castle

- **Hedningarna:** Grodan/Widergrenen; Räven; Tullí; Ukkonen; Juopolle Joutunut; Gorrlaus
- **Imagine Dragons:** Natural
- **J. Rokka:** Marine Migration
- **Jethro Tull:** Jack-A-Lynn; Rhythm in Gold; Overhang; Witch's Promise; No Lullaby; Sweet Dream; Old Ghosts; Dun Ringill
- **John Fogerty:** Old Man Down the Road
- **Kevin Morby:** Beautiful Strangers
- **Loreena McKennit:** The Mummer's Dance; The Mystic's Dream; All Souls Night
- **Low:** Plastic Cup; Witches; Half Light
- **Marconi Union:** First Light; Alone Together; Flying; Always Numb; On Reflection; Broken Colours; Weightless
- **Meditative Mind:** Hang Drum + Tabla Music For Yoga; Hang Drum + Water Drums
- **Motherdrum:** Big Stomp
- **The Notwist:** Hands On Us
- **Orgy:** Blue Monday; Social Enemies
- **Pati Yang:** All That Is Thirst
- **Rob Zombie:** Living Dead Girl; Dragula
- **Rue du Soleil:** We Can Fly; Le Francaise; Wake Up Brother; Blues Du Soleil
- **Saliva:** Ladies And Gentlemen
- **Seether:** Remedy
- **Seth Glier:** The Next Right Thing
- **SJ Tucker:** Hymn to Herne
- **Sharon Knight:** Ravage Ruins; Berrywood Grove; Star of the Sea; Siren Moon; Song of the Sea
- **Shriekback:** This Big Hush; Underwaterboys; The King in the Tree

- **Spiral Dance:** Boys of Bedlam; Burning Times; Rise Up
- **St. Vincent:** Pay Your Way In Pain
- **Steeleye Span:** The Fox
- **Strawberry Alarm Clock:** Incense and Peppermint
- **Tamaryn:** While You're Sleeping, I'm Dreaming; Violet's in a Pool
- **Toadies:** Possum Kingdom
- **Tom Petty:** Mary Jane's Last Dance
- **Trills:** Speak Loud
- **Tuatha Dea:** Tuatha De Danaan; The Hum and the Shiver; Wisp of a Thing (Part 1); Long Black Curl
- **Wendy Rule:** Let the Wind Blow; The Circle Song
- **White Zombie:** More Human Than Human
- **Zayde Wolf:** Gladiator
- **Zero 7:** In the Waiting Line

BIOGRAPHY

New York Times, *Publishers Weekly*, and *USA Today* bestselling author Yasmine Galenorn writes urban fantasy and paranormal romance, and is the author of over one hundred books, including the Wild Hunt Series, the Fury Unbound Series, the Bewitching Bedlam Series, the Indigo Court Series, and the Otherworld Series, among others. She's also written nonfiction metaphysical books. She is the 2011 Career Achievement Award Winner in Urban Fantasy, given by RT Magazine. Yasmine has been in the Craft since 1980, is a shamanic witch and High Priestess. She describes her life as a blend of teacups and tattoos. She lives in Kirkland, WA, with her husband Samwise and their cats. Yasmine can be reached via her website at **Galenorn.com**. You can find all her links at her **LinkTree**.

Indie Releases Currently Available:

Moonshadow Bay Series:
   Starlight Web
   Midnight Web

Conjure Web
Harvest Web
Shadow Web
Weaver's Web
Crystal Web
Witch's Web
Cursed Web
Solstice Web
Dreamer's Web
Woodland Web

Night Queen Series:
  Tattered Thorns
  Shattered Spells
  Fractured Flowers

Starlight Hollow Series:
  Starlight Hollow
  Starlight Dreams
  Starlight Demons

Magic Happens Series:
  Shadow Magic
  Charmed to Death

Hedge Dragon Series:
  The Poisoned Forest
  The Tangled Sky

The Wild Hunt Series:
  The Silver Stag
  Oak & Thorns
  Iron Bones
  A Shadow of Crows

The Hallowed Hunt
The Silver Mist
Witching Hour
Witching Bones
A Sacred Magic
The Eternal Return
Sun Broken
Witching Moon
Autumn's Bane
Witching Time
Hunter's Moon
Witching Fire
Veil of Stars
Antlered Crown

Lily Bound Series
  Soul Jacker

Chintz 'n China Series:
  Ghost of a Chance
  Legend of the Jade Dragon
  Murder Under a Mystic Moon
  A Harvest of Bones
  One Hex of a Wedding
  Holiday Spirits
  Well of Secrets
  Chintz 'n China Books, 1 – 3: Ghost of a Chance,
Legend of the Jade Dragon, Murder Under A
Mystic Moon
  Chintz 'n China Books, 4-6: A Harvest of Bones,
One Hex of a Wedding, Holiday Spirits

Whisper Hollow Series:
  Autumn Thorns

Shadow Silence
The Phantom Queen

Bewitching Bedlam Series:
Bewitching Bedlam
Maudlin's Mayhem
Siren's Song
Witches Wild
Casting Curses
Demon's Delight
Bedlam Calling: A Bewitching Bedlam Anthology
Wish Factor (a prequel short story)
Blood Music (a prequel novella)
Blood Vengeance (a Bewitching Bedlam novella)
Tiger Tails (a Bewitching Bedlam novella)

Fury Unbound Series:
Fury Rising
Fury's Magic
Fury Awakened
Fury Calling
Fury's Mantle

Indigo Court Series:
Night Myst
Night Veil
Night Seeker
Night Vision
Night's End
Night Shivers
Indigo Court Books, 1-3: Night Myst, Night Veil, Night Seeker (Boxed Set)
Indigo Court Books, 4-6: Night Vision, Night's End, Night Shivers (Boxed Set)

Otherworld Series:
> **Moon Shimmers**
> **Harvest Song**
> **Blood Bonds**
> **Otherworld Tales: Volume 1**
> **Otherworld Tales: Volume 2**

For the rest of the Otherworld Series, see website at **Galenorn.com.**

Bath and Body Series (originally under the name India Ink):
> **Scent to Her Grave**
> **A Blush With Death**
> **Glossed and Found**

Misc. Short Stories/Anthologies:
> **The Longest Night (A Pagan Romance Novella)**

Magickal Nonfiction: A Witch's Guide Series.
> **Embracing the Moon**
> **Tarot Journeys**
> **Totem Magick**

Printed in Great Britain
by Amazon

37461609R00116